D1452722

ORIGEN

TREATISE ON THE PASSOVER

AND

DIALOGUE OF ORIGEN WITH HERACLIDES AND HIS FELLOW BISHOPS ON THE FATHER, THE SON, AND THE SOUL

Ancient Christian Writers

THE WORKS OF THE FATHERS IN TRANSLATION

EDITED BY

WALTER J. BURGHARDT
THOMAS COMERFORD LAWLER
JOHN J. DILLON

No. 54

ORIGEN

TREATISE ON THE PASSOVER

AND

DIALOGUE OF ORIGEN WITH HERACLIDES AND HIS FELLOW BISHOPS ON THE FATHER, THE SON, AND THE SOUL

TRANSLATED AND ANNOTATED
BY

ROBERT J. DALY, S.J.

Boston College

PAULIST PRESS
New York, N.Y./Mahwah, N.J.

COPYRIGHT © 1992

BY

THE NEW ENGLAND PROVINCE OF
THE SOCIETY OF JESUS

Library of Congress Cataloging-in-Publication Data

Origen.
   [Peri Pascha. English]
   Treatise on the Passover : and, *Dialogue with Heraclides / Origen* ; translated and
annotated by Robert. J. Daly.
   vi + 121 p. 21.5 x 13.5 cm — (Ancient Christian Writers ; no. 54)
   Translation of: Peri Pascha and Dialogue with Heraclides.
   Includes bibliographical references and index.

   ISBN 0–8091–0452–0
   1. Bible. O.T. Exodus XII, 1–11—Commentaries. 2. Passover—Early works to 1800. 3.
Jesus Christ—Passion. 4. Jesus Christ—Divinity. 5. Trinity—Early works to 1800. 6. Man
(Christian theology)—Early works to 1800. 7. Immortality—Christianity—Early works to
1800. I. Daly, Robert J., 1933–   . II. Origen. Dialogue with Heraclides. English. 1992. III.
Title: Treatise on the Passover. IV. Title: Dialogue with Heraclides. V. Series.
BR60.A35 vol. 54
[BS1245]
270 s—dc20
[230'. 13]   91–33319
                                                         CIP

Published by Paulist Press
997 Macarthur Boulevard
Mahwah, New Jersey 07430

PRINTED AND BOUND IN THE UNITED STATES OF AMERICA

CONTENTS

INTRODUCTION

GENERAL INTRODUCTION

In August, 1941, at Tura, some dozen kilometers south of Cairo, while work was underway to clear rubbish from a limestone cave, formerly a Pharaonic quarry, in preparation for the storage of munitions for the British army, a small papyrus library of works by Origen (ca. 185-251/5) and Didymus the Blind (313-398) was discovered. In all likelihood, they had come from a former Greek monastery, abandoned since the eleventh century, whose ruins are situated on the plateau above the cave. How the codices found their way into the cave can only be conjectured. However, both Origen and Didymus were among those condemned as heretical at the Council of Constantinople in 553, and the condition in which the codices were found (the covers had been removed as if for use elsewhere) suggests that it was not for the purpose of safekeeping and preservation that they were put or thrown into the cave. It is, thus, a logical conjecture that the monks themselves had thrown them there as a way of purging their library of works that had come to be considered heretical or dangerous. The age of the codices, written in a seventh-century Coptic uncial script, is consistent with this conjecture.[1]

The find contained five works or fragments of works of Origen: (1) selections from the Homily on 1 Sam. 28, on the Witch of Endor;[2] (2) selections from Books 1 and 2 of *Against Celsus*;[3] (3) selections from Books 5 and 6 of the *Commentary on Romans*, 3.5–5.7;[4] (4) the *Dialogue of Origen with Heraclides and His Fellow Bishops on the Father, the Son, and the Soul*;[5] (5) the *Treatise on the Passover*.[6]

The last three of these were finds of great significance. Of all this material, we had possessed until now only Rufinus' somewhat suspect Latin summarizing translation (about 400) of the Romans commentary. This discovery has made possible an objective and basically favorable judgment on the reliability of Rufinus' much-maligned translation. The *Treatise on the Passover* and the *Dialogue with Heraclides* had belonged to the large nonextant part of Origen's work. In addition, each of them has a uniqueness that greatly enhances its value. The *Treatise on the Passover*, for example, follows a radically different line of interpretation than most of the other early passover homilies or treatises known to us. The uniqueness of the *Dialogue with Heraclides* consists in the fact that it appears to be a stenographic record of a synod-like meeting of bishops, theologians, and laypeople assembled to discuss and decide on important matters of belief and worship. It is also the only surviving dialogue of Origen. It contains several passages of powerful extemporaneous eloquence which afford us a precious insight into his magisterial theological authority in his own day and into the profound influence he seemed to exercise on those around him. The two works are very typically Origenian in their approach to Scripture, but beyond that, have little else in common—except for the providential fact that they were found at Tura rolled up together, one inside the other, and bound in the middle with a single cord.

Origen's Life and Works

Although it is not always easy to separate hagiographical embellishment from genuine history, especially in what Eusebius, our main source, tells us of Origen's early life, the main outlines are clear.[7] He was born about 185 of Christian parents in Alexandria, where his father was martyred about 201. Precocious in intelligence, and in virtue, too, as the hagiographical accounts relate, by his twentieth year he seems to have already become an instructor of religion, while continuing his study of philosophy and making his living as a teacher of letters.

Sometime before his thirtieth year (ca. 215) he seems to have had a "conversion," after which he devoted himself exclusively to the study and teaching of a "Christian philosophy." This meant, first and foremost, a study of the sacred Scriptures and their role in the life of the Church. By this time he had also visited Rome, probably making the acquaintance of Hippolytus. Upon his return to Alexandria, he took up under Bishop Demetrios the pattern of study, teaching, and writing which was to characterize the remainder of his life. By around 230, at the relatively mature age of 45, he had completed his first works, including what many consider Christianity's first significant attempt at systematic theology: *On First Principles.*

It is quite possible that Origen intended this work to serve, among other things, as an explanation and defense of his theology, i.e., of his spiritualizing and allegorizing methods of interpreting Scripture. However successful in itself, the work certainly did not silence his critics. Several trips followed: to Palestine where he was well received and invited to preach by the bishops of Jerusalem and Caesarea, the latter of whom ordained him in 232 (apparently without the permission and against the at least subsequent protests of Origen's bishop, Demetrios); to Antioch at the invitation of the Empress Julia Mammea, mother of Alexander Severus; and to Athens. During this time his relations with Bishop Demetrios of Alexandria became increasingly strained until there was a complete falling out. Demetrios' protests against the ordination apparently touched only the surface. Origen's adventurous mind and somewhat charismatic stature as Christianity's premier scholar inevitably brought him into conflict with a conservative bishop making strong efforts to solidify the monarchical episcopate in Alexandria. When, by 234, all the dust had settled, Origen had left Alexandria for good and accepted the hospitality and support of the bishops of Palestine, Alexander of Jerusalem and Theoctistus, who had ordained him in Caesarea. He resumed work on the sixth book of his great *Commentary on John,* and apparently spent the rest of his life in Caesarea. In the 17 years between 234 and 251 he produced (by dictation—he is reported to have kept seven stenographers busy) the greater part of a prodigious body of work that is without parallel in patristic literature.

There are some thematic works like the *Treatise on Prayer*, the *Exhortation to Martyrdom*, the *On First Principles*, and the *Against Celsus*; but the overwhelming majority of his approximately 2,000 works are commentaries, homilies, and special investigations on the various books of Scripture.[8] .Nor was this great productivity without its effect; no other patristic figure exercised so much influence and fascination over the great minds that came after him.[9]

Our two works seem to come from the last decade of Origen's activity when he was at the height of his powers, the *Treatise on the Passover* from around 245, the *Dialogue with Heraclides* probably from between the years 244 and 249. There is, apparently, nothing from Origen that can be described as the work of "youth" or of "old age." He seems to have been over 35 before beginning the works for which he is known, and the Decian persecution in 251, in which he was imprisoned and tortured, apparently ended his activity before the onset of any diminishment by reason of age. But whatever the dating, we clearly have here works that can be described as highly typical, even "vintage" Origen.

TREATISE ON THE PASSOVER

The Codex

The codex of the *Treatise on the Passover* consists of 50 pages arranged in three quires of eight sheets (16 pp.) each and a final quire of two sheets (4 pp.) with writing only on the first two of these pages. The pages measure 32 cm. high by 14.4 cm. wide, with columns of writing measuring 22 by 9 cm. There are 35-37 lines per page, with 17-24 Greek characters per line. Insects had left the codex in poor condition, especially the second quire (pp. 17 to 32). In the condition in which it was found, rolled up together with the codex of the *Dialogue with Heraclides*, this second quire was on the outside. The top half of its pages, above the point where the whole roll was tied in the middle with a single cord, are almost completely missing. We have 8 to 15 lines from the bottom half of pages 17-30 and nothing at all from pages 31 and 32. Inside this quire was the first quire (pp. 1 to 16), and inside this the third and fourth quires (33 to 48 and 49 to 50), all in a fairly good state of preservation. Some of these pages are completely intact (see G & N 15-31).

Producing a modern edition of the work promised at first to be the relatively simple task of transcribing and making sense of what could still be rescued from the damaged codex. But then it became clear that much of what was missing could be supplied or at least approximately reconstructed from three different sources: (1) the Greek exegetical catenae, (2) the catena-like commentary on the Octateuch and Kings by Procopius of Gaza (ca. 530), (3) a Latin catena attributable to Victor of Capua (bishop of Capua 541-554).[10] The decision was made to undertake the much more laborious task of reconstructing as well as editing. This was achieved with admirable success by O. Guéraud and P. Nautin, but not published until 1979.

Literary Genre and Central Themes

The *Treatise on the Passover* is not a homily but a treatise (G & N 101-103). It is similar in structure and content to other treatises or homilies written by Melito of Sardis (d. before 190), Apollinaris of Hierapolis (bishop ca. 161-180), Clement of Alexandria (d. before 215), Hippolytus (d. 235-6), and numerous others after Origen. Its two-part structure is similar to what we know of Hippolytus' treatise. Pages 1 to 39.7 comment on the Egyptian passover (Exod. 12.1-11); the second part (pages 39.9 to 50.9) is an exposition of the spiritual meaning of the passover.

Within the context of Origen's work, it appears to have been written *after* 235, the approximate date of Book 10 of Origen's *Commentary on John*, which has an extensive treatment of John 2.13, "the passover of the Jews was at hand," but no mention at all of this treatise. (It was Origen's custom in his commentaries to refer to earlier treatments of the same topic whenever they were relevant or complementary to the topic at hand.) It also seems to come from *before* 248 and Book 9 of the *Commentary on Matthew*, which corrects the erroneous mention of seven barley loaves in *PP* 23.-3 to 24.8. Likely enough, it was also written after the homilies, including the lost homilies on the passover, which seem to have been taken down by stenographers in the early 240s. This helps to explain why Origen's treatment of some verses is so brief. He often did not repeat material he had already presented elsewhere (G & N 108-110).

What occasioned the treatise can only be conjectured. Nautin's suggestion is that it was written in reaction to Hippolytus' treatise (G & N 110-111). Whether or not this constituted the precise occasion for Origen's writing, he takes pains at the beginning of the treatise to point out that he is correcting a false line of interpretation which is followed by "most of the brethren, indeed perhaps all" (*PP* 1.5 to 8). This false line of interpretation, which Origen is at pains to correct, has two interrelated aspects or themes. There is, *first*, the etymology of πάσχα, the Greek word for passover, from the Greek verb πάσχειν = to suffer. This enables one to interpret the passover as a prefiguring of the passion of Christ. Origen is by no means averse to typological or allegorical interpretation, or to developing interpretations from etymologies, but he will not allow such interpretations to run counter to the literal meaning when that meaning is obvious and acceptable and when that meaning suggests another interpretation more consistent with the mystery of Christ. Here in the *PP* he devastates the passover/passion line of interpretation by pointing out that the Hebrew word *pesach* does not mean passion, but passage or passing over, διάβασις or ὑπέρβασις.

This leads us to the *second* theme, which follows from the first and brings us to the very heart of Origen's interpretation of Scripture. He rejects as mistaken, at least in the sense of being incomplete, the traditional idea that the passover is a prefiguring or type of the passion of Christ. For the passion is a historical event; it is a past, completed, and thus no longer "living" event. To interpret Scripture as referring to such an event is, for Origen, not worthy of Christ. Instead, Origen's central insight is that the passover is not a figure or type of the passion of Christ but a figure *of Christ Himself,* of Christ's passing over to the Father (of which the passion was only a historical part) and, by reason of our incorporation into Christ, of our own still ongoing passing over with Christ to the Father.

Each of these two themes is explainable as a strong reaction against the position of Hippolytus and the Quartodecimans (see below), and they do indeed constitute the dominant themes of Origen's treatise. This polemical context also helps to explain why, in an author as consistent as Origen, these two themes are so absent from his treatment of the passover in Book 10 of the *Commentary on John.* The dominant theme there is the "third passover," the one to be celebrated in heaven.

The Early Christian Passover Treatises and Homilies

This literary genre seems to go back to the years 165-170 and the discussions which then arose in the province of Asia and Phrygia between those who celebrated the Christian passover on the Sunday which followed the Jewish passover and a smaller group of bishops who celebrated it at the same time as the Jews on the 14th of Nisan, and hence were called Quartodecimans. Before this, the date of the Christian passover seems not to have been an issue. The growing custom, apparently well established by the end of the second century, of baptizing neophytes as a special part of the passover celebration,[11] helps explain why the topic began to receive so much attention precisely at this time (G & N 96-97).

Melito of Sardis wrote (around 165-170) the first of these treatises known to us. We know of it from an adaptation in homily form written later by someone else. It contains two points important for later developments.[12] (1) It follows the synoptic chronology which locates Jesus' Last Supper at the same time the Jews were celebrating the passover, with the crucifixion taking place the next day. (The Johannine chronology locates the Last Supper on the eve of the Jewish passover.) Hence Melito and his followers argue for celebrating the Christian passover on the same day, relative to the Jewish passover, on which Jesus instituted the Eucharist at the Last Supper. (2) The passover/suffering πάσχα/πάσχειν etymology was used in support of Christians celebrating their passover on the same day as the Jewish passover, the day of the passion, instead of on Sunday, the day of the resurrection, as maintained by the other side of the debate (G & N 97-98).

Apollinaris of Hierapolis (ca. 161-180), wrote a refutation of Melito, enough of which has survived to ascertain the following points.[13] (1) He adopts the Johannine chronology, which implies that Jesus did not eat the passover with the Jews; thus Christians need not follow the Jews for the date of their passover. (2) While following the passover/suffering etymology, knowing no other, he insists that the Jewish passover prefigures the immolation of Christ and not the Eucharist; hence the first Eucharist of the newly baptized need not be celebrated on the day of the Jewish feast.

Clement of Alexandria's treatise on the passover can also be reconstructed sufficiently to establish the following points. (1) Like Apollinaris, he follows the Johannine chronology. (2) But he follows Philo in an etymology which relates passover to a Hebrew word signifying "passage." For Philo, the Jewish passover recalled the Exodus and allegorically prefigured the *passage of the soul* from out of the world of sense into the world of reason.[14] Clement follows this in interpreting the passover as a "passage" out of all passion and everything sensible. But he also Christianizes this in the Pauline sense that Christ himself is the passover (cf. 1 Cor. 5.7). For Clement, this seems to mean that Christ had himself traversed this "passage" by his resurrection, which enables Christians also to traverse it for themselves. This establishes the main line of an "Alexandrian" interpretation which Origen obviously follows and develops (G & N 98-99).

Hippolytus, a contemporary, whom Origen probably came to know personally during his visit to Rome, also wrote a treatise on the passover. This too, like the work of Melito, is known to us in the form of a homiletic adaptation from the pen of a later author.[15] (1) With Apollinaris and Clement, he follows the Johannine chronology, placing the first Eucharist on the eve of the Jewish passover. (2) But he does not seem to be aware of the passover/passage etymology which Philo and Clement followed. Instead, he goes back to the passover/passion etymology of Melito and Apollinaris: "[Christ] did not eat, but suffered, the passover."[16] The homily from which we know Hippolytus' position has two parts. The first treats the Jewish passover in two sections: (a) an account of the first passover in Egypt, and (b) a detailed commentary on Exod. 12.1-15, 43-49. The second part comments on the various episodes of the passion, continuing on through Christ's descent into hell, His resurrection, and His ascension into heaven. This two-part structure provides the apparent model and, as we have already mentioned, perhaps also the concrete occasion for Origen's *Treatise on the Passover*.

However, whatever the historical relationship of Origen to Hippolytus may be, Origen is obviously at pains to counter the position represented by Hippolytus. In addition, the somewhat ungainly structure and disproportionate length of the two parts is easily explainable as a specific reaction against Hippolytus. Origen's first 38 pages constitute a treatise in the form of a commentary on Exod. 12.1-11. He develops the spiritual meaning of these verses as they apply to Christ and to the Christians. The final 12 pages constitute a second treatise, which begins with the announcement that it is going to expound the spiritual meaning of the passover. But this had already been done at some length in the first part. This awkwardness is easily explainable if one assumes that Origen followed this structure in order to make his treatise more obviously a corrective to Hippolytus. Since Hippolytus' second part was largely a treatment of Christ's passion, which Origen wants to avoid in this work, his own second part ends up being disproportionately brief (G & N 99-103).

Origen's Hermeneutics and His
Spiritual Interpretation of the Passover

Origen's theology of the passover is based primarily on his exegesis of Exodus 12. However, it is not based exclusively, and, as we shall see, perhaps not even decisively, on Exodus 12. For what he does here is fully consistent with his general principles of biblical interpretation. He is indeed interested in the letter of the biblical text or, as in this case, the "history" of the Exodus, but primarily because it is a key to the spiritual meaning which lies beneath or behind it. The center of this spiritual meaning is Christ. But this Christ is not primarily the historical Christ or the historical event of Christ's life; it is the *now living* mystical Christ, it is the Christ-event as it is *now* taking place in the lives of the Christian faithful. As Origen himself put it:

> One should not think that historical events are types of [other] historical events, and that bodily things are types of bodily things, but that bodily things are types of spiritual things, and that historical events are types of intelligible events.[17]

It is a genuinely existential interpretation in that the historical "passage" of the Jews from Egypt is seen primarily as a prefiguring of the passage accomplished by Christ and still being accomplished in the souls of the Christians.[18] Origen's interpretation of the Psalms is similarly existential. What is really taking place there is that the eternal Logos is speaking to the Christian who is praying/reading the Psalms.[19] The task of the Christian exegete, then, is to move from the "letter" in order to plumb the mystery of Christ speaking to the soul.

This locates Origen squarely in the Alexandrian tradition of biblical interpretation in general and passover interpretation in particular. For Philo, the Alexandrian Jewish philosopher contemporaneous with St. Paul, the Jewish passover recalled the Exodus from Egypt and prefigured the passage of the soul from the world of sense to the world of reason.[20] Clement of Alexandria, while giving it a Christian development, still follows obviously the same line of interpretation, i.e., the passover was a "passage" beyond every passion and sensible thing. Origen radically Christianizes this, developing a line of interpretation already begun by Clement, by adding, à la 1 Cor. 5.7, that Christ had already accomplished this passage in his resurrection and ascent to the Father, which, in turn, gives to Christians the power to accomplish their passage with him to the Father.

Origen's explicit assertion that "historical" and "bodily" events in Scripture are not figures or types of other historical/bodily (i.e., "dead") events but rather of spiritual and intelligible things/events means that his exegesis follows the same existential structural *pattern* as Philo's. But Origen's is, of course, a baptized or "Christologized" exegesis. The reality prefigured in the Christian is not merely the soul's passage from the bodily to the rational, but also and most especially the passage, made possible by Christ's passage to the Father, of the Christian (or the Christian soul) from the realm of the "bodily-historical" to the realm of the "spiritual-intelligible." One must remember, of course, that for Origen, and especially in the context of passover interpretation, "spiritual" (πνευματικός) and "intelligible " have deeply Christological meanings.[21]

Origen's Interpretation of the Passover
in His *Commentary on John*

About ten years before writing the *Treatise on the Passover*, if our proposed chronology is correct, Origen had already composed a mini-treatise (almost half as long as the *Treatise on the Passover* itself) on the spiritual meaning of the passover while commenting on John 2.13: *The passover of the Jews was at hand.*[22] Both treatments are typically Origenian in approach and method. But in each case Origen has different preoccupations. This results in a relatively small amount of overlapping. In addition, the treatment in the *Commentary on John* ends where the *Treatise on the Passover* begins, with a rejection of the passover/passion line of interpretation.

Origen begins by discussing the meaning of the qualification "passover *of the Jews*" in John 2.13, noting that Scripture elsewhere speaks of the passover *of the Lord* (cf. Exod. 12.11,26,48) or *our passover* (1 Cor. 5.7).[23] Origen interprets this as the distinction Scripture makes between the passover celebrated properly, according to the law (as in Exodus 12), and the passover celebrated by sinners. This, in turn, reminds him of one of his favorite sacrifice texts, 1 Cor. 5.7: *Christ,   our paschal lamb* (or, *our passover*), *has been sacrificed*—τὸ πάσχα ἡμῶν ἐτύθη χριστός.[24] Fascinated by the qualification "*our* passover," Origen offers two explanations:

> To this we must say that he [Paul] simply calls the passover *our passover* because it was sacrificed for us, or that every festival which is really the Lord's (πάσα ἑορτὴ ἀληθῶς Κυρίου)–and the passover is one of these–awaits its consummation not in this age nor upon earth, but in the coming age and in heaven when the kingdom of heaven appears.[25]

Origen makes the second of these interpretations, the idea of the future fulfilment of the passover when the kingdom of heaven has come, the focal point of his attempt to explain the spiritual meaning of the passover. He first quotes Hos. 9.5, Heb. 12.22-33, and Col. 2.16-17 in order to strengthen the idea that we are already involved in this future celebration. Then, after pointing out how complicated and profoundly mysterious this whole question is, and that Paul himself "does not show us to any extent how these things are to be,"[26] he states the question from which everything else develops:

> If there are festivals, among which is the passover, which will also be celebrated in the age to come, it becomes even more necessary to ask how it is that *Christ our passover has been sacrificed* (1 Cor. 5.7) both now and will be sacrificed hereafter.[27]

For not only, Origen observes, do such things as food and drink and new moons and Sabbaths serve as pattern and shadow of the heavenly things to come, but also the festivals.[28]

Origen then lists three objections to the proper understanding of 1 Cor. 5.7 *Christ our passover has been sacrificed*. (1) If the sheep prefigure the sacrifice of Christ, why are the sheep many while Christ is one? (2) How explain that the sheep are sacrificed by observers of the law, but Christ by transgressors of the law? (3) How can one apply to Christ the specific prescriptions in Exod. 12.8-10 on how to eat the flesh of the lamb? Pleading lack of space, he takes up only the third objection, claiming thereby to be answering the others by way of summary. His first step is, significantly, to quote John 1.29:*This is the Lamb of God, who takes away the sin of the world*. He asserts that this is referred to in Exod. 12.5, showing, in effect, that John, "agreeing with Paul here, seems to be struggling with the same difficulties which we are examining."[29] Like his treatment of John 2.13 in Book 10, Origen's treatment of John 1.29 in Book 6 is also a mini-treatise. Other than the *Treatise on the Passover*, it constitutes the richest single passage on the theme of sacrificial soteriology known to us in Origen's extant works.[30] The somewhat abrupt insertion of John 1.29 at this point of the *Treatise on the Passover* suggests that he wants us to recall that earlier treatment of it. There seems to be no doubt that Origen sees the spiritual meaning of the passover (or of Exodus 12) as inextricably intertwined with 1 Cor. 5.7 and John 1.29, for all these texts are speaking about the same reality. He then plunges into the heart of the matter:

> *If the Word became flesh* (John 1.14), and the Lord says: *Unless you eat the flesh of the Son of Man and drink his blood, you have no life in you; he who eats my flesh and drinks my blood has eternal life, and I will raise him up on the last day. For my flesh is food indeed, and my blood is drink indeed. He who eats my flesh and drinks my blood abides in me, and I in him* (John 6.53-56), **then** the flesh thus spoken of is that of the Lamb who takes away the sin of the world (cf. John 1.29); and this is the blood, some of which was to be put on the doorposts and lintel of the houses in which we eat the passover (cf. Exod. 12.7), and it is necessary to eat the flesh of this lamb in the time of the world, which is night (cf. Rom. 13.12; 2 Peter 1.19). And the flesh roasted with fire is to be eaten with unleavened bread (cf.

Exod. 12.8). For the Word of God is not just flesh; for He Himself says: *I am the bread of life* (John 6.48) and: *This is the bread which comes down from heaven, so that someone may eat of it and not die. I am the living bread which came down from heaven; if anyone eats of this bread, he will live forever* (John 6.50-51b). Yet one must not forget that, loosely speaking, all food is called bread; for it is written of Moses in Deuteronomy: *For forty days he ate no bread and drank no water* (Deut. 9.9) instead of "he took no food, solid or liquid." I make this point because in the Gospel of John it is said: *And the bread which I shall give is my flesh for the life of the world* (John 6.51c).[31]

This passage is a typical illustration of the way Origen will move quickly from one biblical book to another and across the two Testaments. This is not due to any disregard for the differences between the various books of Scripture. Indeed no one in antiquity was more knowledgeable and sensitive than Origen in this regard. It is due rather to his conviction that, no matter how varied and different the Scriptures may be, they all point ultimately to the same reality: Jesus Christ and the life in Christ lived by his followers.[32]

Origen continues his spiritual interpretation by commenting that we eat the flesh of the Lamb with bitter herbs and unleavened bread when we sorrowfully repent of our sins and take the occasion of setbacks to return to the contemplation of truth.[33] Next, the command to eat the flesh not raw or boiled but roasted (Exod. 12.9a) is interpreted as a command to avoid the slavery of the letter and to convert the rawness of Scripture into food cooked in the divine fire, so that those who in fervent spirit[34] and with a good life partake of this well-cooked flesh of the Lamb may be able to say, as Christ speaks in us (cf. 2 Cor. 13.3): *Our heart was burning within us on the road while he opened to us the Scriptures* (Luke 24.32).[35]

Origen then interprets the command to eat the different parts of the lamb, the head symbolizing the most elevated doctrines about heavenly realities, the feet symbolizing the more mundane or even underworldly realities, the entrails symbolizing the more esoteric and hidden realities (cf. Exod. 12.9b). The prohibition against breaking any bones of the lamb (from Exod. 12.46, but included in 12.9 by the LXX) signifies the divine command not to offend against "the unity of the Spirit that is in all the Scriptures."[36] The command to let none of the lamb remain until morning reminds us that this prophecy of the lamb of which we have been speaking is useful nourishment to us only as long as the dark night of this life lasts (cf. Rom. 13.12; 2 Peter 1.19). When this night has passed we will have the unleavened bread which has nothing to do with the old leaven of here below, and which will serve us until we are given the manna, the bread of angels and not of men (cf. Ps 78[77].25).[37] Origen then rounds off his main discussion of the spiritual meaning of the passover with the remarks:

> Each of us, therefore, can sacrifice the lamb in every one of our family homes, and while it is possible for one to break the law in not sacrificing the lamb, it is possible for another to observe the commandment entirely in sacrificing it and cooking it thoroughly and not breaking a bone of it (cf. Exod. 12.10 LXX). And thus, in brief, in harmony with the apostolic interpretation [or: the interpretation of the Apostle] and with what the Gospel says of the lamb, is how one must interpret the passover which was sacrificed (cf. 1 Cor. 5.7). For one shouldn't think that historical events are types of [other] historical events, and that bodily things are types of bodily things, but that bodily things are types of spiritual things and that historical events are types of intelligible events.
>
> However, as for lifting up our mind to a discussion of the third passover which is to be celebrated in *festal gathering with innumerable angels* (Heb. 12.22) in the most perfect and most blessed exodus,[38] this is not necessary here; we have already spoken of these things to a greater extent than required by the passage at hand.[39]

After another page of remarks on the significance of Capernaum, and of the fact that only in John is the passover mentioned at the beginning of the Gospel, and after putting off to another occasion a discussion of the date of the passover,[40] Origen closes by vigorously rejecting the interpretation of Heracleon that the passover was a type of the passion:

> And yet Heracleon says: "This was the great festival, for it was a type of the passion of the Savior; not only was the lamb put to death, but the eating of it afforded repose, while the sacrificing of it pointed to the passion of the Savior in the world, and the eating of it to the repose in the wedding to come." We have quoted him in order that, seeing how incautiously and inconsistently and without any proof the man proceeds in such an important matter, we will know better how to disregard him.[41]

Since Origen is willing to accept Heracleon's insights when they are helpful, the force of his rejection of Heracleon on this point is striking. The passover/passion interpretation alone does not account for this vehemence, for "most of the brethren," (including Hippolytus, whom he seems to have highly respected), as Origen will later admit at the beginning of the *Treatise on the Passover*, seem to follow this line of interpretation. But some of the vehemence, which is conspicuous in an otherwise dispassionate passage, can be accounted for by the fact that this interpretation contradicts the more true and much more vitally important etymology and interpretation of the *passover as passage*. The antitype of the passover cannot be for Origen anything this-worldly, not even something as sacred as, in the words of Heracleon, "the passion of the Savior in this world." The true antitype, the that-to-which everything literal or this-worldly or historical points, must be fundamentally other-worldly— "spiritual—πνεματικός," as Origen would put it. In this case it is the "passage" of Christ (and, bound with this, the passage of the Christian) to the Father.

But there is also another reason which helps account for the emotion which seems to be latent in this particular refutation of Heracleon. "The repose in the wedding to come–ἀνάπαυσις ἐν γάμῳ," to which Heracleon refers the eating of the lamb in the third passover in the world to come, is a technical term used by the Gnostics to signify the reunion of the pneumatic element with the original Pleroma.[42] The mere mention of this would be enough to discredit vehemently, even by mere association, Heracleon's (in itself less objectionable) passover/passion interpretation.

This serves as a convenient transition to the *Treatise on the Passover*. Summing up this introduction, we can say that it was not simply the fact that others interpreted passover as "passion" instead of "passage" that motivated Origen to write his passover treatise as he did. It was rather because he had a very different conception of the spiritual meaning of scripture than these others, and because one or other of these conceptions tended to prevail depending on whether one followed the "passion" or the "passage" interpretation.

Outline of Origen's *Treatise on the Passover*

The numbering refers to the codex pages and lines. Thus, *PP* 7.15 = codex page 7, line 15. For pages 17 to 30, where there is no top of the page from which to count, a minus sign before the line number indicates that one is counting *from the bottom* of the codex page. Thus 23.-10 refers to codex page 23, 10 lines from the bottom. To avoid confusion, we use the preposition *to* instead of a dash (e.g., 22.1 to -5) to refer to passages of more than one line in length.

Conclusion **49.34 to 50.8**

Manuscripts, Editions, and Translations

Our sole textual witness for the *Treatise on the Passover* as a whole is the unique codex described above. It is listed as Papyrus No. 88746 in the Museum of Egyptian Antiquities in Cairo. It is accessible only through the single critical edition: O. Guéraud and P. Nautin, *Origène: Sur la Pâque* (Christianisme antique 2; Paris: Beauchesne 1979) . This edition provides an extensive introduction (pp. 15-150), the Greek text (transcribed as found in the codex, with its gaps reconstructed as far as possible from the several patristic catenae described above) with facing French translation and notes (pp. 154-253), a Scripture index and an index of Greek words (pp. 255-272) . Our translation follows closely the arrangements and divisions of this edition. Our notes to the translation are, for the most part, a selection from its extensive material. As far as we know, the *Peri Pascha* has not yet been translated into any other language.

DIALOGUE OF ORIGEN WITH HERACLIDES AND HIS FELLOW BISHOPS ON THE FATHER, THE SON, AND THE SOUL

In addition to what has already been presented in the general introduction and in the introduction to the *Peri Pascha* about the Tura papyrus discoveries and about the life and work of Origen, the following additional remarks will suffice to introduce the *Dialogue with Heraclides*.

The Codex

There are 28 pages arranged in two quires of eight sheets or 16 pages (like the *Treatise on the Passover*). After p. 28, the next two pages are blank and the final blank half-sheet is missing. The pages measure 32 cm. high and 29.8 wide, which makes them much wider than those of the *Treatise on the Passover*. There are between 30 and 39 (averaging 34) lines per page, usually with some 27/28 Greek characters per line. The codex, rolled up inside the quires of the *Treatise on the Passover*, was found in almost perfect condition.[43] Unfortunately, however, it represents a stenographic report which was apparently never corrected by Origen himself, and which the original scribe, in a number of places, obviously did not understand or report clearly. In a number of these instances, a second or third hand has made additions or emendations (some of which are attempts to improve already existing emendations), but, as it seems, not very helpfully.[44] The modern editors and translators (J. Scherer, H. Chadwick, E. Früchtel) generally find the original version a better basis for attempting to make sense of confused or apparently incomplete passages. In our translation and comments, we make use of these previous efforts. In points of doubt, we favor Scherer, the original modern transcriber/editor/translator of the text.

Literary Genre

The work seems to be the record of a synod-like meeting of bishops, in the presence of lay people, called to discuss matters of belief and worship. Origen appears as the obvious, authoritative leader in the discussion. The first two pages consist of an intense question-and-answer dialogue in which Origen tactfully but firmly brings Heraclides to a more acceptable formulation of the unicity of God which does not deny the distinct existence or divinity of Jesus, the Son. It is a fascinating picture of a church struggling to steer a safe course between the Scylla of monarchianism and patripassianism, towards which Heraclides seems to incline dangerously, and the Charybdis of ditheism, towards which Origen seems to incline. This was, of course, long before the Church had struggled its way to the clarifications and definitions that enabled it to secure the faith against what it came to recognize and reject as subordinationism, Arianism, Sabellianism, Apollinarism, and the other Christological and trinitarian heresies.

But after the first two pages, the dialogue effectively ceases. Heraclides does not appear again. There is an intervention by Maximus (6.8), a question from Denis (10.20), and a remark by Demetrius (24.24). Otherwise it is all Origen: explaining, instructing, and even preaching. He does this as an authoritative teacher of Christianity to whom even bishops go to school and humbly subject themselves to his questioning. There are indications that some, and perhaps even a considerable amount, of preliminary matter is missing. That may explain why the question-and-answer part of the *Dialogue* is so brief. Quite possibly, these two pages represent the summary of a long series of discussions, or perhaps a summarizing conclusion to the discussions over the point at issue, now "staged" as it were for the benefit of the full assembly before all the people. In any case, these first two pages seem to serve primarily as an introduction to the teaching of Origen on a number of currently pressing theological problems.

This is the only surviving dialogue of Origen. There are indications that suggest that it may have been copied from a collection of Origen's dialogues in the library at Caesarea. We do not know what was in this presumed collection, but we do have indications from other sources at least about the following dialogues, debates, or discussions: from about 215 with the governor of the province of Arabia; towards 229 with the Valentinian Candidus (apparently a head-to-head debate); a similar debate later with Bassus; in the winter of 231-232 before the empress mother Julia Mammea; at the Synod of Bostra (between 238-244) with the bishop Beryllus; and finally, another synod-like meeting with bishops in Arabia (modern-day Jordan), which seems to have been conducted in a manner similar to what we find in this dialogue. There also seem to have been discussions or disputations with Jewish rabbis.[45]

Outline and Central Themes of the Dialogue with Heraclides

PART ONE

PART TWO

PART THREE

The *Dialogue* begins with Heraclides stoutly professing his faith, which apparently had been called into question, in the divinity of the Word. Origen then leads him by a series of questions to a more acceptable formulation of this faith. This more acceptable formulation, however, is the easily misunderstood, and to monarchian sensibilities rather shocking, "We profess two Gods" (2.26). Origen thus has to explain how God is both one and two at the same time (2.28 to 4.19). Next comes the practical matter, which may have been the concrete starting point of the whole problem in the first place, of how one is to offer the (official, public) prayer of the Church.[46] The answer is: not *just* to the Father, but specifically, "to God . . . through Jesus Christ by reason of his communication in divinity with the Father" (4.30 to 32). This section (4.19 to 5.10) concludes with a plea that the conventions (in public prayer, presumably) be adhered to.

Then, without pausing, Origen takes up an anticipated objection: the relation of the divinity of Christ to the resurrection (5.10 to 6.7). In a fine example of his method of sewing together various biblical texts to make his point, he emphatically affirms the physical reality of Christ's body (i.e., it is not just a spiritual body), and hence the bodily reality of Christ's resurrection and ours. This leads to an intervention by Maximus, seeking clarification on the mode of Christ's resurrection.[47] Origen's answer centers on the role played by the *spirit* of Christ in the resurrection, in the context of the tripartite composition (à la 1 Thess. 5.23) of human beings *and* the human Jesus.[48] Origen emphasizes that the human Jesus has the same composite elements—body, soul, spirit—as we do; otherwise we would not be wholly saved. Illustrating the synthetic wholeness of his Christian vision—theory and practice, faith and works are never far apart in his mind—Origen ends Part One of the *Dialogue* with a homiletic exhortation to right conduct as well as to correct belief (8.21 to 10.19) .

To Origen's question whether any other matters of faith need to be discussed, Bishop Denis asks what was apparently a familiar, unsettled question: "Is the soul blood?" Origen's answer, constituting Part Two of the *Dialogue* (10.20 to 24.24), is a good illustration of his method of exegesis as well as of some of the problems connected with it. The problem at hand arises from the literal meaning of the Septuagint of Lev. 17.11, supported by Deut. 12.23: *the soul* (ψυχή) *of all flesh is its blood.* This was apparently suggesting to some that the soul was material and thus subject to corruption with the body in the grave. Origen points out that Scripture often uses bodily things to describe spiritual realities. But his real answer is to insist that the question cannot be answered directly, on its own terms, but only in its larger context as part of the mystical order in which the *interior human being* is understood as that human being which is *in the image and likeness of God.* Origen now interrupts his instruction with an impassioned plea to his audience (12.19 to 15.24) not to make him guilty of casting pearls before swine. He knows from sad experience that the literalists who will misunderstand and stomp on the truth (and those preaching it) are found not only among the Gnostics and Jews but also among the simple faithful.[49] Because of them he should not go on; but if he does not go on, those capable of receiving the truth will be defrauded of it. Origen feels himself on the painful horns of a practically insoluble dilemma which has already caused him much grief in his life. He does go on, of course, relating the Pauline doctrine of the interior human being (Rom. 7.22; 2 Cor. 4.16; Col. 3.9-10) to the Gen. 1.26 account of the human being created *in the image of God.* The exterior human being mentioned by Paul refers to the *other*, bodily human being whose creation is related in Gen. 2.7. The original question about soul/blood is thus sublated in the overall synthesis in which each part of the exterior human being has its corresponding part, and homonym, in the interior human being.[50]

Such exegesis and its results became profoundly influential in the development of Christian theology. But as we now look back on it, we can identify at least two fundamental problems connected with it. (1) Antedating modern historical-critical methodology, Origen (with his contemporaries) often had no access to the clear literal meaning of the biblical text. For example, he does not know that the problem in the question "Is the soul blood?" comes from translating the Hebrew *nephesh* (life-principle, essence-of-life, etc.) by the Greek ψυχή (soul, as opposed to body and spirit), and from assuming that the common, Hellenized concept of the nature and composition of the human being was what the Pentateuch (for him, Moses) had in mind. (2) There are thus many places where the biblical text does not yield a satisfactory literal meaning. This means that he must search for the spiritual meaning. In this search, his particular Hellenistic-Platonic-Christian view of human and divine reality, without his being aware how much this view of reality differs from that of the biblical authors, becomes codeterminative of the spiritual meaning he finds in the biblical texts.[51]

Origen ends this section with an impassioned prayer to be dissolved and be with Christ, professing his readiness even for martyrdom in order to achieve this end. At this point, a natural end to the piece, Bishop Philip arrives and Bishop Demetrius tells him that Origen has been teaching that the soul is immortal. Origen does not want to let this go without comment, so we have another few pages which comprise Part Three (24.24 to 28.23). Origen's comment centers around a distinction between the three kinds of death: (1) death to sin, when we live to God; (2) death to God, when a soul sins; (3) the ordinary (μέσον) death when we leave our bodies, or are dissolved. All human beings die, but no human *soul* ever dies this third death. The *Dialogue* ends with another impassioned prayer expressing Origen's yearning *to be away from the body and at home with the Lord* (cf. 2 Cor. 5.8).

Manuscripts, Editions, and Translations

The sole textual witness is the unique codex listed as Papyrus No. 88745 in the Museum of Egyptian Antiquities in Cairo. It is accessible through the critical edition: J. Scherer, *Entretien d'Origène avec Héraclide et les évêques ses collegues sur le Père, le Fils et l'âme* (Publications de la Société Fouad I de papyrologie; Textes et documents 9; Cairo: Institut français d'Archéologie orientale 1949). This edition is essentially reproduced with Greek text and French translation, but without the transcription of the codex and most of the technical paleographical discussion, in J. Scherer, *Entretien d'Origène avec Héraclide* (*SC* 67; Paris: Cerf 1960). There is a German translation with extensive notes by E. Früchtel, *Das Gespräch mit Herakleides und dessen Bischofskollegen über Vater, Sohn und Seele. Die Aufforderung zum Martyrium* (Bibliothek der griechischen Literatur 5; Stuttgart: Anton Hiersemann 1974). There is an English translation with brief introduction and notes by H. Chadwick, *Alexandrian Christianity: Selected Translations of Clement and Origen with Introductions and Notes* (Library of Christian Classics; London: SCM/Philadelphia: Westminster 1954) 430-455. There is also an excellent study in Italian which gives special attention to the rhetoric, style, and even "eloquence" of Origen: Gennaro Lomiento, *Il dialogo di Origene con Eraclide ed i vescovi suoi colleghi sul Padre, il Figlio e l'anima* (Quaderni di "Vetera christianorum" 4; Bari: Adriatica 1971).

The codex is clear and easily readable. But in many places the meaning it carries is garbled or incomplete. Each of the above-mentioned editors/translators has made helpful suggestions on the meaning of doubtful passages. But these suggestions do not always agree. Serious scholars will have to make their own study, for we can give only fleeting attention in our notes to some of these doubtful passages.

TREATISE ON THE PASSOVER
(Peri Pascha)

Introduction: the Name of the Passover

1   Before beginning a word-for-word exegesis of the passover, a few words about the mere name of the passover are
5 in order. Most of the brethren,[1] indeed perhaps all, think
that the passover (πάσχα) takes its name from the pas-
10 sion (πάθος) of the Savior.[2] Among the Hebrews, however, the real name of this feast is not πάσχα but *fas*—the
15 three letters of *fas* and the rough breathing, which is
much stronger with them than it is with us, constituting
the name of this feast which means "passage" (διάβασις).[3] For since it is on this feast that the people come out
20 of Egypt, it is thus called *fas*, that is, "passage" (διάβασις). Because it is not possible in the Greek language to
25 pronounce this word the way the Hebrews do, since the
Greeks are unable to pronounce *fas* with the stronger
breathing in force among the Hebrews, the word was Hel-
30 lenized: in the prophets it is called *fasek*, and when Hellenized more completely, the word becomes πάσχα. And
should one of us in conversation with Hebrew people too
rashly mention that the passover takes its name from the
35 suffering of the Savior, he would be ridiculed by them as
2   one totally ignorant of the meaning of the word. They
presume of course that they, as perfect Hebrews, have the
proper interpretation of the name of the passover.[4]
5   Now this should be enough comment on the mere name
10 to teach us the meaning that comes from the word *fas* and
to warn us against rashly attempting to interpret things

27

15 written in Hebrew without first knowing the Hebrew meaning. We come now to an examination of the text itself, knowing that the passover (πάσχα) means passage (διάβασις).

The Passover of the Departure from Egypt

20 When the Hebrew people came out of Egypt, it was fitting that the law was given to them to celebrate the feast 25 in this way: that, *house for house, they are each to take a perfect male lamb without blemish* (cf. Exod. 12.3-4; Lev. 22.19) and sacrifice it, and that *towards evening;* (Exod. 12.6) they are to *eat it roasted with fire, not raw nor boil-* 30 *ed in water* (Exod. 12. 8-9), so that *the destroyer of the first-born of the Egyptians* (Exod. 12.23; cf. Heb. 12.28) *would not touch any of them when he saw the lintels* of 35 their doors sprinkled with *blood* (Exod. 12.7,23). After 3 this the people leave Egypt and the first-born of the Egyptians perish, and Pharaoh, after the exodus of the Hebrews, changes his mind and goes out in pursuit of them with his army and his chariots and is thus drowned 5 in the Red Sea, but Moses passes through the sea with the people.

10 That the passover still takes place today,[5] that the sheep (πρόβατον) is sacrificed and the people come up out of Egypt, this is what the Apostle is teaching when he 15 says: *For Christ, our paschal lamb, has been sacrificed. Let us, therefore, celebrate the festival, not with the old leaven, the leaven of malice and evil, but with the un-* 20 *leavened bread of sincerity and truth* (1 Cor. 5.7-8). If *our Passover has been sacrificed, Jesus Christ,* those who sacrifice Christ come up out of Egypt, cross the Red Sea, and 25 will see Pharaoh engulfed. And if there are any among you who would like to return to Egypt, they will not enter into the Holy Land.[6] But that the meaning contained in the historical events might be more clearly demonstrated

to the mind,[7] we will now come to the text itself, word for word.

The Lord said to Moses and Aaron in the land of Egypt.
35 *"This month shall be for you the beginning of months; it shall be the first month of the year for you"* (Exod. 12.1-2)

This month is the beginning of months

4   God says to Moses and Aaron that this month is the *beginning of months* and is also *the first month of the year*
5 for them when they leave Egypt. As far as the history goes, this month is indeed the *first month,*[8] and the Jews
10 celebrate this festival each year *on the fourteenth of the first month* (cf. Exod. 12.6; Num. 9.3) by sacrificing a *lamb in each household* (Exod. 12.3) according to the law given
15 them through Moses. But when Christ came *not to abolish the law or the prophets but to fulfill them* (Matt. 5.17), he showed us what the true passover is, the true "passage"
20 (διάβασις) out of Egypt. And for the one in the passage, *the beginning of months* is when the month of passing over out of Egypt comes around, which is also the beginning of ano-
25 ther birth for him—for a new way of life begins for the one who leaves behind the *darkness and comes to the light* (John 3.20-21)—to speak in a manner proper to the sacra-
30 ment (σύμβολον) through water given those who have hoped in Christ, which is called the *washing of regen-*
35 *eration* (Titus 3.5). For what does rebirth signify if not the beginning of another birth?

For you[9]

          One must enter into a perfect state of life and a perfect
5 love in order to be able to hear, while still in this present world, the words: *This month is* for you *the beginning of*
5 *months*. For this is not said by God to the whole people, but only to Moses and Aaron. For it is not written: "And
10 God said to the people: This month is for you the begin-

ning of months; it is the first month of the year for you."

15 Rather, it is written: *The Lord spoke to Moses and Aaron
in the land of Egypt, saying: This month is for you the beginning of months; it is the first month of the year for you.*

20 Then he adds: *Speak to the whole assembly of the sons of
Israel and say: On the tenth day of this month they shall*

25 *each take a lamb* (Exod. 12.1-3). If he had added: "Speak
to the whole assembly of the sons of Israel and say: This
month is for you the beginning of months," he would have
been saying this without distinction both to Moses and

30 Aaron and the whole people. But since it is *to Moses and
Aaron* that it is said: *This month is for you the beginning
of months; it is the first month of the year for you*, and

35 since he (Moses) is ordered not to say this, but that *on the

6   tenth day of the month* they should *take a lamb according to their fathers' houses* (Exod. 12.3), it is clear
that it is not for the whole people that that month was

5 then *the beginning of months*, but only for Moses and Aaron
to whom it was spoken. For it is necessary to have completely renounced creation and this world to understand

10 that one has become almost other than what one was in
order to be able to hear: *This month is* for you *the beginning of months: it is for you the first month of the year.* For

15 the fact that the perfect man has the beginning of another
birth and becomes other than what he was, this is what
the Apostle is teaching us when he says: *The old man in us*

20 *was crucified with Christ* (Rom. 6.6), and again: *If we
have died with him we shall also live with him* (2 Tim.
2.11; cf. Gal. 2.19), and then speaking boldly of himself: *It*

25 *is no longer I who live, but Christ who lives in me* (Gal.
2.20); these are the kinds of people who can, while still in
the world, hear that *the first month* and *the beginning of*

30 *months* has come to pass for them. Let us now look into the
fact that it is when the perfect person becomes other than
what he was, that he then receives from God His prom-

35 ises and blessings (ἐπαγγελίας καὶ εὐλογίας). It is not *Ab-*

7   *ram* who receives the promises, but *Abraham* (cf. Gen.
     17.5); and it is not *Jacob* who receives the blessings, but
     Israel (Gen. 32.28-29); it is not *Simon* who becomes the first
5   disciple of the Savior, but *Peter* (cf. Mark 3.16; Matt. 16.
     17-18); *James and John* are not sent as apostles until they
     have become *Boanerges, that is, "sons of thunder"* (Mark
     3.17). No matter where we look, we find things of this
10   kind everywhere in the Scriptures pointing out that those
     who have been made perfect have new names because they
     are no longer the same but have become other than what
     they were.

"Beginning" and "first"[10]

15   This is how *the beginning of months* comes to pass for
     them. But it is good to know [. . . whether *beginning* and
20   *first* mean the same thing or two different things . . .],[11]
     but *This month is for you the beginning of months: it is*
25   *the first month of the year for you.* He could have said:
     "This month is for you the first of the months of the
30   year," or: "This month is the first month of the year for
     you." But since there is a difference, he says that the
     month is the beginning and that it is the first. What,
8   then, is the way we should take to come to understand
5   whether *beginning* and *first* are used as equivalent terms
     or for different things except by being guided by similar
     passages found in the Scriptures?

     Right at the beginning of the creation account, it says:
10   *In the beginning God created the heaven and the earth*
     (Gen. 1.1). Now the Scripture knows that there is a differ-
     ence between *first* and *beginning*; thus it does not say:
15   "First He created." For since the creation had the demi-
     urge as its beginning, but was not the first work done by the
20   demiurge, for the demiurge made many other things as
     well[12] *   *   *[13] (it is not this creation that has the charac-
     ter of being *first*). But the things which were made did

25 have a *beginning*, although logically they may be either
first or second. For, properly speaking, *first* applies only
when nothing comes before, and *beginning* applies to those
30 things which are beginning even if they come last. What
is *first* is always *beginning,* but *beginning* is not always
first.

But to come to a better understanding of this statement,
35 let us take an example which will lead us to its meaning.
9 If a builder who had never built a house begins to build,
5 we would find this house-building to be both the *first* and
the *beginning.* For since he had never built anything,
when he does build it, it would then be his first building,
10 for he had never built a house before this. However, even
if this is the first house he builds, it is, while still being
15 the first, also the *beginning*. Thus, *beginning* refers to the
foundation, but it is also *first* since he is building it as his
20 first house. If it is the second or third house which he
builds, * * *14 (it obviously has a *beginning*, since it begins with its own *beginning*; but this is not the house
which has the quality of being *first*), for this (the first)
25 would then be the house built before this and in the first
place.

To understand this more clearly, let us take another ex-
30 ample: If several pieces of wood lie side by side, we will
find for each of them its *beginning*–for each of them–but
only the one which occupies the first place is the *first*. It
35 is on the one hand *first* because it occupies the first posi-
10 tion, and it has on the other hand its own *beginning*, and
each of those that follow, while excluded from being *first*,
has its own *beginning*.

5 Now then, since *beginning* is not in every way *first*, but
first is in every way *beginning*, the Scripture says that
10 this month is for them *the beginning of months* and *the
first month of the year*. And that this might not seem to be

a mere affirmation, let us again call to witness the Savior
15 who teaches us that there is a distinction between *beginning* and *first*. For in the Apocalypse attributed to John
the Savior says: *I am the Alpha and the Omega. the first*
20 *and the last, the beginning and the end* (Rev. 22.13). * * 15
For (just as there is a great) difference between (*alpha*)
and *omega*, and just as the *beginning* is different from the
25 (*end*), so too *first* (and *last* are not) the same thing, and it
becomes obvious that *beginning* is used for one thing and
first for another. But since it has been shown that the first
30 is also necessarily the *beginning*, this logically says that
he who is *first* is also *beginning*: for *I am*, he says, *the*
first and the last, the beginning and the end (Rev.
35 22.13). For inasmuch as he is *the first-born of all creation*
11 (Col. 1.25), he is *first*, and inasmuch as he is wisdom, he is
beginning.   For this is what Wisdom says through the
mouth of Solomon: *The Lord created me at the beginning of*
his ways (Prov. 8.22).

5   And this is probably what John had in mind when he
began his Gospel with the words: *In the beginning was the*
10 *Word, and the Word was with God, and the Word was*
God. He was in the beginning with God (John. 1.1-2). He
takes the *beginning* to signify Wisdom, and says that the
Word is not "beginning" but *in the beginning*. For when the
15 Son is with the Father in his own proper glory (cf. John
17.5), he is not said to be *first*, for this belongs to the
Father alone, for God alone is unbegotten (ἀγέννητος). The
Son is not *first* . . .

* * * [lines 19 to 26 missing]

                          . . . (but inasmuch as he) rules all
things with wisdom, he is the *beginning*. That is why,
30 when he comes into the world, John does not say: "First
was the Word," but: *In the beginning was the Word*.
    Jacob, who had become Israel, also used this distinction
35 between *first* and *beginning* when blessing Reuben: *Reuben*
is my first-born and my strength and the beginning of my

12 *children* (Gen. 43.3). For he knew that Reuben was both his *first-born* and the *beginning* of his *children*.

5   In the Scripture will be found many such things which, to those who read superficially, will seem to be identical,
10 but which, to those who read with care and attention, will reveal their differences. For if (the Scripture) says: *The foolish and the senseless will perish together* . . . (Ps. 50[49].10). * *

* * * [lines 12 to 16 missing]

17 The Apostle indicates (a distinction of the same kind) when he (says) . . .

* * * [lines 18 to 24 missing]

The passover is not a type of the passion[16]

25 . . . the lamb (πρόβα[τ]ον) is sacrificed by the saints or the Nazirites,[17] while the Savior is sacrificed by crimi-
30 nals and sinners. And if the passover lamb is sacrificed by saints, and if the Apostle has said: *For Christ, our pas-chal lamb, has been sacrificed* (1 Cor. 5.7), then Christ is sacrificed according to the type (τύπον) of the passover,
13 but not by the saints, and thus the passover is indeed a type of Christ, but not of his passion (καὶ τύπος μὲν Χ(ριστο)ῦ ἐστιν τὸ πάσχα, οὐ μέντοι γε τοῦ πάθους
5 αὐτοῦ). It is necessary for us to sacrifice the true lamb–if we have been ordained priests, or like priests have of-
10 fered sacrifice—[18] and it is necessary for us to cook and eat its flesh. But if this does not take place in the passion of the Savior, then the antitype of the passover is not his
15 suffering; rather the passover becomes the type of Christ himself sacrificed for us. For each one of us first *takes* the *lamb* (12.5), then dedicates it, then sacrifices it, and thus,

20 after *roasting* it (12.9), eats it and after eating it *leaves*
nothing until the morning (12.10), and then celebrates the
feast of unleavened bread (12.17) after having come out of
Egypt. To show that the passover is something spiritual
25 and not this sensible passover, he himself says: *Unless you*
eat my flesh and drink my blood. you have no life in you
30 (cf. John 6.53). Are we then to eat His flesh and drink His
blood in a physical manner? But if this is said spiritually,
then the passover is spiritual, not physical.

14   Let us now see whether what was said by the Savior
follows what was written in the law of the passover. For
just as it is written there that whoever does not eat the
5 passover *shall be cut off from his people* (Num. 9.13), now
the true Lamb says that whoever *does not eat his flesh*
10 *does not have life* (cf. John 6.53). Just as *the destroyer* then
was not able to touch those who ate of the lamb (cf. Exod.
12.33; Heb. 11. 28), so now whoever eats of the true lamb
escapes the *destroyer*.[19]

        But if . .

* * * [lines 15 to 21 missing]

                                              . . . as we
said above (13.1), the passover is not a type of the passion
25 but a type of Christ Himself.—For the Savior Himself
says: *As Moses lifted up the serpent in the wilderness, so*
must the Son of Man be lifted up (John 3.14) in accord with
30 the type of the serpent *hung on the wood* by Moses (cf.
Num 21.8-9; Deut 21.22-31), indicating nothing less than
the passion of the Savior *hung on the wood*—it is obvious-
35 ly in accord with the type of the serpent and not in accord
15   with the type of the passover that one will understand
5 the passion.[20] For if he had said: "Just as Moses performed
the passover in Egypt, so too must Christ suffer," it would
be incontestable that the passion took place as antitype
10 of the passover. But since He likened his passion to the

serpent hung on wood, His passion cannot be the antitype of anything but this . . . * * *

[lines 12 to 25 missing]

　　　　　　　　　　　　. . . perhaps it is not for all that Christ is sacrificed and was crucified, but for those who
30　can say: *To me the world has been crucified and I to the world* (Gal. 6.14), and for those who can say: *He disarmed the principalities and powers and made a public example*
35　*of them, triumphing over them on the wood (of the cross)*
16　(Col. 2.15), and for those who can say: *Far be it from me to glory except in the cross of our Lord Jesus Christ, by which the world has been crucified to me and I to the world* (Gal.
5　6.14).[21] But we come now to the following text:

　　Tell all the congregation of the sons of Israel that on
10　*the tenth day of this month they shall take every man a lamb according to their fathers' houses, a lamb for a household* (Exod. 12.3).

How the Hebrews celebrate the Passover[22]

　　He does not say: "On the tenth day of the month they
15　should sacrifice a lamb" but: *They should take a lamb.* They are ordered to sacrifice this lamb *on the fourteenth* (Exod. 12.6), and this is how the Hebrews perform the
20　passover: Beginning on the tenth day they must take a lamb, *house by house* and *family by family*, continue to
25　feed it themselves on the eleventh and twelfth and thirteenth, and dedicate it saying: "this lamb is sacrificed
30　for so and so," not going beyond fifty names, and *on the fourteenth* sacrifice it *between the two evenings* (Lev. 23.5) so that there are five days from the taking of the
17　*Cat*　lamb until its sacrificing. This is how the sensible (αἰσθητόν) passover took place.

Take it on the tenth

* * * [lines 4 to -10 missing][23]

-10 that the true Lamb is Christ because of the fact that,
being second after the Father, he is taken—I am speaking
of the number ten[24]—during the second monad.

Keep it until tbe fourteenth[25]

-5 And just as there the lamb is not sacrificed at the same
time as its taking on *the tenth*, but *on the fourteenth*, five
days later, so also here

18 Cat *when one has taken* (cf. Exod. 12.3-5) the true Lamb,
that is, Christ, one does not immediately sacrifice
5 and eat him but after an interval of five days from
his *taking*. For when someone hears about Christ
and believes in him he has *taken* Christ, but he
10 does not sacrifice or eat him before five days have
gone by (cf. Exod. 12.3,6). For since there are five
senses in the human being, unless Christ comes to
each of them, He cannot be sacrificed and, after
15 being roasted, be eaten. For it is when *he made clay*
-19 *with his spittle*

and *anointed* our *eyes* (John 9.6-7)) and made us *see clearly*
-15 (Mark 8.25), when He *opened the ears* (cf. Mark 7.33-35) of
our heart so that *having ears* we can *hear* (cf. Matt. 11.15;
13.19), when we smell his *good odor* (cf. Eph. 5.2; 2 Cor.
1.15), recognizing that his name is a *perfume poured out*
-10 (Cant. 1.3; cf. Phil. 2.7), and if, *having tasted*, we *see how
good the Lord is* (cf. 1 Peter 2.3; Ps. 34[33].8), and if we
touch him with the touch of which John speaks: *That
-5 which was from the beginning, which we have heard,
which we have seen with our eyes and touched with our
hands, concerning the word of life* (1 John 1.1), then it is
that we will be able to sacrifice the lamb and eat it
19 Cat and thus come out of Egypt.

* * * [about 25 lines missing]

having often observed . . .

* * * [almost 2 lines missing]

-5 . . . Psalm 8 was entitled: On the Wine Vats (cf. LXX). So
too when the temple was built, a certain number was given
for the burden-bearers and the hewers of stone who
20   worked on it: *70,000 burden-bearers and 80,000 hewers of
stone* (1 Kings 5.15).

* * * [about 18 lines missing]

-15   . . . we have come out.
There are other words like this which show it to be pre-
-10 scribed by law that the passover lamb is to be sacrificed *in
the first month, on the fourteenth of the month, between
the two evenings* (Lev. 23.5), when the light of the moon
has become full and perfect. For the lamb was sacrificed *on
-5 the fourteenth day of the month. between the two evenings,* when, beginning with the fifteenth day, the sphere
of the moon reaches its fullest plenitude
21 *Pr*   in the opinion of the experts.
       Cat   And for our part, unless the perfect, true light (cf.
5   John 1.9) rises over us and we see how it perfectly
illumines our guiding intellect, we will not be able
to sacrifice and eat the true Lamb.

* * * [about 15 lines missing]

A lamb for each household

For in telling his disciples to have the crowd *on the
grass* (Luke 9.13-14; Mark 6.39; Matt 14.19) he says:
-10 *Make them sit down by companies* (Mark 6:39; John 6.10),
and that is how they are served. For it not by indiscrim-
inately gathering the crowds which eat his bread, but by
-5 gathering them into homogeneous groups that he serves
them.[26] In addition, the phrase which follows (Exod. 12.4)

has practically the same meaning as what has just been
explained.

22   *But if there are too few in the household to be enough
for a lamb, one is to take along with himself his neighbor*
5 *who lives next to him. according to the number of persons,
each one is to be counted towards a lamb according to what*
10 *each can eat. Your lamb shall be without blemish, a male
a year old; you shall take it from the sheep or from the
goats* (Exod. 12.4-5).

One is to take along with himself his neighbor
who lives next to him

*   *   *   [about 11 lines missing]

(Since) *one will take along his neighbor so that* the
-10 household is *enough for a lamb*, it is right to say that *one
counts towards a lamb*.

A lamb without blemish, a male, a year old

A lamb without blemish, a male, a year old.[27] For
Christ is a *perfect* being, since there is *nothing lacking* or
5 deficient in him. Male indicates his firmness and courage.
And it is said to be a year old because the year signifies a
completed number

23   *Pr*   since the sun returns to its own place after an interval of twelve months.

Taken from the sheep or the goats[28]

5 *Pr*   And those who eat do not all eat in the same way
but differently, each according to his own capacity;
for they cannot all partake of him as lamb but some,
10 and perhaps most, only as *goat*. Those then who are
perfect and already making every effort to be without sin, they eat of what is *taken from the sheep*,
15 because Christ is the *Lamb of God who takes away
the sin of the world* (John 1.29);

but the others who still lie subject to sin will take it *from*
-10 *the goats,* because one is told in the law to offer a goat as a
sacrifice *for sin* (cf. Lev. 4.28; Heb. 10.18; Lev. 16.6-10,
15-22).

Perhaps the Gospel has knowledge of the same distinc-
-5 tion when the Savior feeds his followers not with the
same but with different bread. Because for some he breaks
five loaves of wheat, and for others seven loaves of barley,[29] so that those who

24 Pr cannot partake of Christ as purest *bread* of wheat
5 because they are of beastly nature and do not yet
live spiritually (λογικῶς) will partake of him as
barley bread.
And since people of this kind are more
10 numerous, there are seven barley loaves, because this is
the number both of fulness and of idleness, in accordance
with which lives the most numerous crowd; their hands
15 are idle and they do not *work until the day comes* (cf. John
9.4). The loaves of wheat bread are five,
-15 as are also the senses in which those who are spiritual do
not suffer hunger but keep their senses ever nourished by
-10 the spiritual (λογικῷ) bread, as it is written: *They shall
hunger no more, neither thirst any more. nor will their
eyes grow weary* (cf. Rev. 7.16-17; Isa. 5.27),[30] and so forth.

-5 *And you shall keep it until the fourteenth day of this
month, when the whole assembly of the sons of Israel
shall kill it towards evening. And they shall take some
25 of its blood and put it on the two doorposts and the lintel
of the house in which they eat them* (Exod. 12.6-7).

The whole assembly of the sons of Israel shall kill it
5 ### towards evening

Cat It is towards evening (cf. Exod. 12.6b) that we are
ordered to kill the lamb, since it is at *the last hour*

10   (1 John 2.18) that the true Lamb, the Savior, *has
            come into the world* (cf. John 1.9).[31]

The application of blood to the houses

-15   . . . which we sacrifice, and which we anoint with blood,
      our *houses,* which is to say, our bodies, which anointing is
-10   the faith we have in him, by which faith we have confi-
      dence in the destruction of the power of the *destroyer* (cf.
      Exod. 12.23). And after we have been anointed, that is,
 -5   after having believed[32] in Christ, we are then ordered to
      move on to the eating of Christ, as the following words
      show.

            *They are to eat the flesh the same night, roasted   with
      fire, and they are to eat unleavened bread with bitter*
26   *herbs. Do not eat any of it raw or boiled with water, but
      roasted with fire, the head with the feet and   the entrails*
      (Exod. 12.8-9).

Eat the flesh roasted with fire

* * * **[about 4 lines missing]**

5 *Cat*   If the lamb is Christ and Christ is the Logos,
             what is the flesh of the divine words if not the di-
10   vine Scriptures? This is what is to be eaten *neither
             raw nor cooked with water*. Should, therefore, some
             cling just to the words themselves, they would eat
15   the flesh of the Savior *raw*, and in partaking of this
             raw flesh would merit death and not life—it is
             after the manner of beasts and not humans that they
-15   are eating his flesh—since the Apostle teaches us that
      the letter kills, but the Spirit gives life (2 Cor. 3.6). If the
-10   Spirit is given us from God and *God is a devouring fire*
      (Deut. 4.24; Heb. 12.29), the Spirit is also fire, which is
      what the Apostle is aware of in exhorting us to *be aglow*

-5 *with the Spirit* (Rom. 12.11). Therefore the Holy Spirit is rightly called *fire*, which it is necessary for us to receive in order to have converse with the *flesh* of Christ, I mean the divine Scriptures, so that, when we have roasted them with this divine *fire*,

27   *Cat*   we may eat them roasted with fire. For the words
  5   are changed by such fire, and we will see that they are sweet and nourishing.

Unleavened bread with bitter herbs

* * * [about 20 lines missing]

Not raw or boiled with water[33]

-10 . . . after having drunk of this water, *out of their heart will flow rivers of water* (John 7.38) *welling up to eter-*
-5 *nal life* (John 4.14). However, the Savior criticizes the water of the Samaritan woman, saying: *Everyone who drinks of this water will thirst again* (John 4.13); but this water He praises, saying: *Whoever drinks of the water*
28 *that I shall give him will never thirst.*

* * * [about 19 lines missing][34]

. . . We are commanded not to *cook* the flesh of the Savior, that is, the word of Scripture, with such a *water*, and
-10 not to mix with the words of Scripture another material which could water it down in the cooking, but to partake
-5 of it by cooking it with *fire* alone, that is, with the divine Spirit, and *not* eat it *raw or cooked with water*.

For the Jews partake of them *raw* when they rely on just the letter of the

29   *Cat*   Scriptures. But if through the Spirit they see the true circumcision, if there really is a circumcision,
  5   and the true Sabbath, and *work while it is day* before *the night comes, when no one can work* (John

9.4), they are already eating the word *cooked* with the Spirit.

* * * {about 16 lines missing]

> . . . firmness
> . . . watery, so that
-5   . . . by the Spirit
> . . . by the flame and
> . . . are burned
> . . . participate
> . . . of those who eat

30   * * * [about 21 lines missing]

The head with the feet and the entrails

-15 *Pr*   . . . some partake of its *head*, others of its hands, others of its breast, others also of its *entrails*, still
-10   others of its thighs, and some even of its *feet*, where there is not much flesh,
each partaking of it according to his own capacity. Thus it
-5 is that we partake of a part of the true Lamb according to our capacity to partake of the Word of God. There are
31 some who partake of the head and, if you wish, of each part of the head,
Pr   for example, of the ears so that, *having ears*, they
5   can *hear* his words (cf. Matt. 11.15; 13.9,43). Those who *taste* of the eyes *will see* clearly (cf. Ps 34[33].9; Heb. 6.4-5) *lest you dash your foot against a stone* (cf. Ps 91[90].12; Jer. 13.16; Matt. 4.6; Luke 4.11). Those who taste the hands are the *workers* (cf. John
10   9.4) who no longer have *drooping hands* (Heb. 12.12) which are *closed against giving* (cf. Sir. 4.31), the ones who accept correction before *the Lord becomes*
15   *angry* with them (cf. Ps. 2.11). Others, *resting on its breast* (cf. John 13.25), will even recognize from this food who the betrayers of Christ are (cf. John 13.21-

20   26).³⁵ The studious who eat of the entrails will see
      even to the depths of God–for the entrails have a
      certain harmony of twists and turns and they also
      make for the body everything needed for life; and
      such function of one initiated in the mysteries (ἐν
25   μυστηρίοις)–or rather they see the hidden ratio
      (λόγον) of the Incarnation situated as it were in the
      middle, at least if we take the head to be the divin-
      ity.³⁶ All those who partake of the thighs keep
30   their flesh *undefiled, following wherever* Christ
      should lead (cf. Rev. 14.4). And they who partake
      of the feet, *hesitant* no longer, run *in haste* (cf. Rom.
35   12.11) *toward the prize of the upward call of Christ*
      (Phil. 3.14). It is also possible that the head is
      faith and feet the *works* without which *faith is
      dead* (Jas. 2.17).

32   Varied indeed is the food
    Pr   of those who eat the passover, but they are *all one*
5   (cf. Acts 2.44); even he who eats the head is one
          with whoever eats the feet, since *the head* cannot
          say to the feet: "I have no need of you." For the
          members eaten are *many* but *the body of Christ is*
10   *one* (1 Cor. 12.20-21). Let us preserve, then, as well
          as possible the harmony of the members in order not
          to incur the reproach of dividing the *members of*
          Christ (1 Cor. 6.15).

15   *You shall let none of it remain until the morning, and*
      you shall break no bone of it. What remains of it until
      morning shall be burnt with fire (Exod 12:10).

Leave nothing until morning³⁷

20 *Vic*   Just as the mysteries of the passover which are
          celebrated in the Old Testament are superseded by
          the truth of the New Testament, so too will the
          mysteries of the New Testament, which we must

25   now celebrate in the same way, not be necessary in
the resurrection, a time which is signified by the
morning in which *nothing will be left, and what
does remain of it will be burned with fire.*

You shall break no bone of it[38]

* * * [several lines missing]

33   we partake of the flesh of Christ, that is, of the divine
Scriptures. . . .

* * * [lines 3 to 13 missing]

. . . of the true Lamb, for the Apostle professes that the
lamb of our passover is Christ when he says: *For Christ,*
20   *our paschal lamb, has been sacrificed* (1 Cor. 5.7); his
flesh and blood, as shown above, are the divine Scrip-
25   tures, eating which, we have Christ; the words becoming
his bones, the flesh becoming the meaning from the text,
30   following which meaning, as it were, *we see in a mirror
dimly* (1 Cor. 13.12) the things which are to come, and the
blood being faith in the gospel of the *new covenant* (cf. 1
35   Cor. 11.25; Luke 22.20), as the Apostle attests in the following words: *And profaning the blood of the covenant*
34   (Heb. 10.29). In anointing ourselves with his blood, which
is faith, we will escape the destroyer (cf. Exod. 12.23).
And if an uneducated person . . .

* * * [lines 3 to 9 missing]

What remains until morning shall be burned with fire[39]

10   *For our knowledge is imperfect and our prophecy is imperfect,* as the same Apostle teaches, *but when the perfect*
15   *comes, the imperfect will pass away* (1 Cor. 13.9-10), this
is what the Scripture says is *burned in the morning.* The
night is taken for the present world (cf. Gal. 1.4) and the

day for the world to come (cf Matt. 12.32; Eph. 1.21) as the
20 same Apostle attests, saying: *The night is far gone, the
day is at hand* (Rom. 12.13). But only a very *few* (Matt.
22.14) are *they who have their faculties trained by prac-*
25 *tice to distinguish good from evil* and who can take *solid
food* (Heb. 5.12,14) and who will be capable of *not leaving
any flesh until the morning,* as the Scripture says, per-
30 haps *one in a thousand* or *two in ten thousand* (cf. Eccl.
7.28; Sir. 6.6; Deut. 32.30), among whom were the blessed
apostles.

And the Scripture describes the behavior of those who
eat the passover in the following words:

In this manner you shall eat it: Your loins girded, your
35 *sandals on your feet, and your staff in your hand; and you
shall eat it in haste. It is the Lord's passover* (Exod.
12.11).

Your loins girded

5   What it means to have one's loins girded we will learn
from other passages of Scripture. The Apostle, explaining
what has come from the *loins of Abraham* blessed by Mel-
10 chisedek (Heb. 7.5,10), says this: *Even Levi, who receives
tithes, paid tithes, for he was still in the loins of his
father when Melchisedek met him* (Heb. 7.9-10); and in
15 another place he says: *Although they came from the
loins of Abraham* (Heb. 7.5); and in Job, Scripture says of
the devil: *His strength is in his loins and in the navel of*
20 *his belly* (cf. Job 40.16); for it is especially through this
appetite that the devil can confuse and overcome human
beings, the *loins* being taken as a polite expression for the
25 male, and the *navel of the belly* for the female, in order to
show that it is especially through this appetite that he
gets control over the male and the female.

30   With Scripture thus attesting that the *loins* are there
for copulation, we are on the way to understanding why,
35 with regard to the passover, it wants us to eat *in family
groups* (Exod. 12.21) and *with our loins girded*. We are
36 ordered, whenwe eat the passover, to be pure of bodily
sexual union, for this is what the girding of the loins
5 means. Thus Scripture teaches us to bind up the bodily
source of seed and to repress inclinations to sexual relations
when we partake of the flesh of Christ. For if an athlete

* * * [4 lines defective]

                                        . . . competing and keeping
15 his eyes fixed on those who for a *perishable* prize *exercise self-control* only *to receive* a *perishable* prize, while
he himself is struggling to receive an *imperishable* prize
20 (1 Cor. 9.20-25). For if one girds his loins in this way, he
will also be able *not to leave any of the meat until morning* (Exod. 10.12,46).

       Perhaps this is the reason why John the Baptist, since
25 he was perfect, had a *girdle of leather around his loins*
30 (Matt. 3.4), to show that he had mortified there every
       genital instinct of his body, the *leather* indicating mor-
tality because mortality permeates his whole nature. And
35 the married man who eats the passover will also gird his
37 loins; for blessed are *they who have wives as if they did
not have them* (1 Cor. 7.29), said the Apostle.[40]

Sandals on your feet

5   It says also that those who eat the passover have sandals on their feet, which to some might seem to be contrary to the oracle delivered to Moses. For when Moses
10 trod on holy ground, he was ordered to take off his sandals. How is it, then, since the passover is also holy, that
15 those who eat it are ordered to put on their sandals? How-

ever, these points are not in conflict but refer to different
20 things. When one walks on *holy ground* (cf. Exod. 3.5), one
is ordered to be clothed with nothing mortal, since there
will no longer be anything mortal to conceal; but when one
25 eats the passover, one is ordered to eat in haste in order to
be ready, as the Apostle teaches when he says: *having
your feet shod in readiness to preach the gospel* (Eph.
30 6.15).[41] In order to be able to go forth expeditiously at the
break of *day* (cf. Rom. 13.12), the command is given to be
shod; and herein lies a fairly clear indication relating to
35 the resurrection of the flesh: it is that the flesh itself also
goes out with us as we depart from Egypt. For we must *put
38 *to death what is earthly in us: immorality, impurity. li-
centiousness, idolatry*, and so forth (cf. Col. 3.5; Gal. 5.19-
20) and thus depart from Egypt.[42]

Your staff in your hand

5   And that we might see the similarity between the law
and the Gospel, we will juxtapose what was said in the
10 law with the words of the Gospel. When Moses was about
to lead the people out of Egypt in order to bring them into
the Holy Land, as he was receiving the commandments
15 from God he was ordered to have no shoes on. Also the
apostles, being sent to lead the people of the Gentiles out
of the spiritual Egypt, are ordered to *take no staff for the
journey, nor bag, nor be shod with sandals* (Mark 6.9; Matt.
20 10.10). Just as they in Egypt who eat the passover *in haste*
are ordered to have *sandals on their feet*, so also in the
25 Gospel, to those who are already able to sacrifice and eat
the passover, as indicated above (cf. 37.33), the Apostle
gives the command, as to those who have already *girded
30 their loins with truth and put on the breastplate of
righteousness* and *taken the helmet of salvation*, that
they should henceforth also be *shod in readiness to preach
the gospel* (cf. Eph. 6.14,15,17), and that they should
henceforth also have *staffs in their hands* (cf. Exod.

12.11)[43] as ones who are to share henceforth in the task of
39   training, because the staff is the symbol of training. For
    5 *he who spares the rod hates his son, but he who loves him*
      is diligent to discipline him, as we have read in Proverbs
      (Prov. 13.24).[44]

II

Introduction: the Spiritual Meaning of the Passover[45]

Since the sacred ceremony and sacrifice of the passover
    10 was already carried out in mystery (μυστηριωδῶς) in the
      time of Moses according to God's orders for the salvation of
      the first-born of the sons of Israel because of *the wrath of*
    15 *God inflicted* (cf. Rom. 3.5) on Pharaoh and on those who
      under his leadership disobey the word of God, we now
      raise the question whether it is only in that time of its
    20 concrete celebration that it is carried out, or whether we
      might not have to admit that it is also carried out in a
      different manner in our own time, the time of fulfillment–
      upon whom the end of the ages has come (1 Cor. 10.11). In
      answer to this we have found that the sacred and inspired
40   Scriptures are not silent; we find that they oblige us to ful-
      fil the commands which have been given, and that they
    5 have been fulfilled up to our time, according to the word:
      Search the Scriptures, in which you have life, and they
    10 *give witness of me* (cf. John 5.39). And their witness does
      not consist only in words of prophecy, but in the very acts
      themselves knowledge is written. This is what the great
      prophet, in full understanding, ordains for the Hebrew
    15 nation when he envisions the taking and the keeping of
      the lamb, and then its sacrificing and its eating after
      being roasted, and the manner of clothing, and the haste
    20 in consuming what had been sacrificed; and the burning up
      of the remains, and the fulfillment of the commandment
    25 that this should be done *forever in the generations* to come
      as a memorial for them *and their sons* (cf. Exod. 12.14,24);

for he recognizes there not only the historical but also the
30 anagogical meaning, as it is written: *interpreting spiritual
truths to those who possess the Spirit* (1 Cor. 2.13).

I will therefore try, with the grace of God, to expound
35 the spiritual meaning in order that the power of salvation accomplished in Christ may become manifest to those
who love instruction, as it is written: *To all who received*
41 *him, he gave power to become children of God; who were
born, not of blood nor of the will of the flesh nor of the
will of man, but of God* (John 1.12-13). For adoption in
5 Christ has given us the power of so tremendous a salvation, we who are not born of the blood and the will of man
and women, and whom He [Christ] recognizes as His
10 brothers when he says: *I will proclaim thy name to my
brethren* (Heb. 2.13; Ps. 22[21].23).

The Passover Lamb, Figure of Christ

For these, salvation has been brought about by the
15 blood of Christ himself *like a lamb without blemish* (Isa.
53.7; cf. Lev. 23.12 etc.). For it is written: *Like a lamb he
was led to the slaughter, and like a sheep that before its
20 shearers is dumb, so he opened not his mouth. Who will
recount his generation, that he is cut off out of the land
25 of the living, and led to his death for the transgressions
of his People? And I will give the poor in exchange for
30 his grave, because he committed no sin and there was no
deceit in his mouth* (Isa. 53.7-8; cf. Acts 8.32-33). For it was
not because *of sin* that his death came about, but *he him-
35 self bears our sins and suffers for us and by his bruises we
have all been healed.*

42 For just as they [the Hebrews] were prefigured in a
male lamb (cf. Exod. 12.5), so are we in the *man like a
lamb* (cf. Isa. 53.7); just as they were prefigured in a per-
5 fect lamb (cf. Exod. 12.5), so are we in the *fullness* (cf. John

1.16) of him who has carried out his Father's will; just as
they were prefigured in a one-year-old lamb, so are we *at
the end of the ages* (1 Cor. 10.11)–for just as the year is the
10 fulfillment of the months, so is he the fulfillment of the
law and the prophets–just as they in a lamb *without
blemish* (cf. Exod. 12.5 etc.), so we in a man without sin;
15 just as they in the *first month* (cf. Lev. 23.5), so we in *the
beginning of all creation, in which all things were made*
(cf. Rev. 3.14; Col. 1.15-16; [there] *in the tenth month* (cf.
Exod. 12.3), [here] in the fullness of the unicity [of God].[46]
As for the words *up to the fourteenth* (cf. Exod. 12.6), a
20 number of the second week, this signifies a repose[47] of two
weeks which came between the first creation, i.e., the
invisible one, and the second creation, the visible one.[48]

25   *The whole assembly of the sons of Israel* shall slaughter it *towards evening* (cf. Exod. 12.6); *all the assembly of
the sons* of "the man who sees God,"[49] i.e., of a "power"[50]
30 of God. *Towards evening* towards *the end of the ages*
(1 Cor. 10. 11). And they will anoint *with its blood the lintel and the two doorposts* (cf. Exod. 12.7); the *lintel* is that
35 which is above the head of all the members of the flock;
43   the *doorposts* are the boundaries through which they [the
passions] enter among and depart from the Sons of Israel—
5 some of them go in and others go out—and within which
they are contained when they dwell among them.[51]

The Conduct of Those in Passage[52]

The sacrifice takes place in Egypt, where Pharaoh
holds sway, a country which is of earth and oppressed
10 with darkness,[53] and which signifies ignorance. Those who
are under the power of this ruler of Egypt are in a profoundly ignorant state of blindness; and he [Pharaoh],
15 having set himself up there, is possessed of a swollen
opinion of himself which made him say: *Who the Lord is
I do not know, and I will not let Israel go*, which is equiv-
20 alent to saying: *I will set my throne above the clouds; I*

*will climb up into heaven; I will be equal to the Most
High* (cf. Isa. 14.13-14).

Therefore, those who heed the prophet will celebrate
25 this passover as strangers in his [Pharaoh's] land, as
having come under his tyranny in a time of *famine* (cf.
Amos 8.10-11), because they received from their fathers
30 that very old oath made to their father, Abraham, that
his *descendants would be sojourners* (Gen. 15.13).[54] For the
sacrificing of this lamb was carried out by them in ignorance because *they do not know what they are doing*–and
35 that is why *it is forgiven them*–(cf. Luke 23.34). For it is
44   good *that one man die for all the people* (cf. John 18.14).
For it is not permitted for *a prophet to die outside Jerusalem* (Luke 13.33), i.e., apart from those who try to live
in peace and justice.[55]

5   Just as they who were subject to the law, and who, for
not fulfilling even what was required by the law, fell
from the natural salvation that comes through the law. . .
[copyist's omission] . . . after having received the command to celebrate it [the passover] according to the law.
10 These are the ones who, in the *haste* (cf. Exod. 12.11) of
faith and in the stifling of corporeal thoughts and in the
careful *putting on of their shoes* (Exod. 12.11) in prepara-
15 tion for the journey of doing good, with their *staffs* held
ready *in their hands* (Exod. 12.11), conduct their lives
thenceforth *in fear* (1 Peter 1.17) which becomes salvation
20 for them. And *If you do not eat my flesh and drink my
blood, you have no part in me* (John 6.53; 13.8).[56]

This is what the true Sheep says, who is truly the
Lamb who *takes away the sin of the world* (John 1.29),
25 who *alone dies* so that the whole human race might be
saved according to the word of the *high priest of that
year* who was speaking without knowledge (cf. John 11.45-
30 52). For the sacrifice was prepared for the salvation of

those who, by reason of the childishness of their love for
the earth which nursed and reared them,[57] are called
35 sojourners. Because they were nursed by the earth they
treated it as their mother, not knowing their true mother,
yielding to the licenses of the flesh, after having been
45 brought up in familiarity with their bodies and with this
quite pleasurable *transient* (cf. 2 Cor. 4.18) world, and af-
5 ter having been swayed by ignorance of their inherited
world.[58]—And these are called Hebrews. For it is said:
The God of the Hebrews has summoned us (Exod. 5.3). For
10 when the migrant world has passed over into the firmly
established age of the Father,[59] the return of the children
comes about because of the actual realization of the name
15 of the passover which is called "passage—ὑπέρβασις,"
for they pass over by means of the name of this mystery,
after having participated in it, obtaining for themselves
20 the salvation of not being exterminated with the *first-
born of the Egyptians from Pharaoh, who sits upon his
throne, even to the first-born of the maidservant who is
behind the mill* (Exod. 11.5; cf. 12.29), i.e., with those who
25 in the pride of wealth and tyrannical power are in ignorance and do not recognize Him who *raises up* kings *from
the dust and makes them sit on royal thrones* (cf. 1 Sam.
30 2.8). For he has given . . . **[copyist's omission]** . . con-
fined by ignorance within the boundaries proper to each
one, some by fate, others by fortune, others by the power of
35 the Prince[60] because of the nurturing in conformity with
him which they received in the time of childhood, hav-
46 ing forgotten their natural mother and their true Father
who says: *I have indeed seen the affliction of my people
in Egypt, and I have heard their cry and I have come*
5 *down to deliver them from their taskmasters and to
deliver them* from the slavery of Pharaoh and *from the*
10 *hand of the Egyptians and* to *lead them into the land of
their fathers which I promised to Abraham and to Isaac
and to Jacob, to give to them as an inheritance* (Exod. 3.7-8;
15 6.8; cf. Gen. 48.21; 50.24), and this is what he did *at the
end of the age* when he came *to put away sin by his flesh*

20 *in putting enmity to death; and having come he pro-*
claimed the good news to us who are far off and to us who
are near, delivering us from the dominion of darkness and
25 *establishing* us *in his light* (Eph. 2.16-17; Col. 1.12-13; 1
Peter 2.9; etc.).[61] For he did indeed set us free from Egypt
and its leaders whom *he nailed to the cross to make a pub-*
30 *lic example of them, triumphing over them in the cross* (cf.
Col. 2.14-15). This is why he says: *Behold I come—for it*
is written of me in the head of the book—O God, to do thy
will (Heb. 10.7-8; Ps. 40[39].7-8); for it is prophesied: *Sac-*
35 *rifice and offering you did not want, but a body you have*
prepared for me; in burnt offering and sin offerings you
47 *have taken no pleasure* (Heb. 10.5-6; Ps. 40[39].7). By this
offering of himself the world which has gone astray is pu-
5 rified and converted,[62] and he *pacifies* all things *in the*
blood of his cross by putting to death hostility (cf. Eph.
2.16), i.e., the *wrath* which leads to the destruction *of the*
disobedient (cf. Rom. 2.8). For if they were eager to obey
10 what was said in the ordinance, carrying out the ceremony
with a *bunch of hyssop* (cf. Exod 12:22), i.e., with a sacrificial fragrance (ἀναθυμιάσει) of thoughts on conversion,
15 that was for them the realization of the true passover of
Christ, who says: *For these I consecrate myself, and not for*
these alone but for all those who believe in you (John 17.
20 19-20). For it is not in faith that they set out to celebrate
the perfect passover but in non-faith, without full knowledge of the Scriptures[63] which the prophets proclaimed.
As Scripture says: *If you do not believe, neither will you*
25 *understand* (Isa. 7.9). *For I have come not to do my will but*
that of him who sent me (John 6.38), and this will was
that He be given for all those who believe.

Eat it in haste: it is the Lord's passover (Exod. 12.11b)[64]

For if this haste of theirs had the effect of bringing
30 them to offer sacrifice for their consecration (cf. above
47.14 to 17), they would then have fulfilled the command-

ment which says: *Eat it with haste; it is the Lord's passover* (Exod. 12.11), i.e., the passage (ὑπέρβασις) of the
35 Lord. For the one person who has passed beyond the limits
fixed by God because of the disobedience of Adam, this one
48 person is indeed the Lord who has blunted the *sting of
death* (1 Cor. 15.55) and suppressed its power, giving by
5 his gospel preaching a mean of escape *to the spirits imprisoned* in hell (cf. 1 Peter 3.19; 4.6), and also by provid-
ing them with a means of ascent into heaven, by means of
10 His own ascent, after opening the gates and portals by
means of His own entrance: *Lift up your gates, O princes,
and be lifted up, O ancient doors, and the King of glory
will enter in* (Ps.24[23].7,9). And after this command was
15 heard a second time by the powers stationed at the
gates,[65] and when they asked *who is there, they heard:*
20 *The Lord strong and mighty in battle, the Lord of hosts,
this is the King of glory* (Ps. 24[23].8,10), for He is *the
King* of the Father's *glory* in which the Father is glori-
25 fied, *reconciling the world to himself, not counting its
trespasses against it* (cf. 2 Cor. 5.19), but *having cancelled
the bond which stood against it with its legal demands,
this he set aside* (Col. 2.14). And this he did in Christ, as
30 Scripture says: *For God was in Christ reconciling the world
to himself* (2 Cor. 5.19, and the reconciliation took place
according to the prophecy: *Like a blameless lamb led to
the slaughter, I was in ignorance.* For they [the powers of
35 hell] were devising an *evil plot against him* (cf. Jer. 11.
19), knowing the text: *It is necessary for the Son of Man to
49 suffer much and be put to death and on the third day to
rise again* (cf. Matt. 16.21; Mark 8.31; Luke 8.22). And as
the disciples, on hearing this, were somewhat grieved, He
5 said: *It is good for you that I go away* (John 16.17); for *the
grain of wheat, unless it die, remains alone; but if it die, it
10 bears much fruit* (cf. John 12.24), which agrees with the
text: *Here am I and the children God has given me. Since,
therefore, the children share in flesh and blood, he him-
15 self likewise partook of the same nature, that through
death he might destroy him who has the power of death,*

*that is, the devil, and deliver all those who through fear
of death were subject to lifelong bondage* (Heb. 2.13-15).
20 For they *were freed from the servitude of the world ruler
of this present darkness* (cf. Eph. 6.12) by the true Lamb
25 who is Christ Jesus, of whom the lamb slaughtered in
Egypt was the true type, when he delivered the Hebrews
of that time from the power of the one governing Egypt—
which means darkness, Pharaoh—which means dissipat-
30 er, because he dissipates the works of virtue done in the
light by means of his princely power, i.e., by the thought
of those who live in darkness.[66]

Conclusion

This is all that I can say. May God, after planting
50 within you fruitful beginnings through these pen scratch-
es, grant that what we have said briefly and inadequate-
5 ly may be brought to full completion by those who love re-
flection and study.[67] Just as the Logos has assisted us, so
may God assist them according to the same gift of grace in
Christ.

The Passover Treatise of Origen

DIALOGUE OF ORIGEN WITH HERACLIDES AND HIS FELLOW BISHOPS ON THE FATHER, THE SON, AND THE SOUL

1   **Dialogue Of Origen wlth Heraclides and His Fellow Bishops on the Father, the Son, and the Soul**

5   When the bishops in attendance had expressed their worries about the faith of the bishop, Heraclides, so that he would profess before all what he believed, and after each had expressed his opinion and asked his questions, Heraclides said:

10   "I too believe what the holy scriptures say: *In the beginning was the Word. and the Word was with God, and the Word was God. He was in the beginning with God: all things were made through him, and without him was not*

15   *anything made that was made* (John 1.1-3). Thus we share the same faith. In addition we also believe that Christ took flesh, that He was born, that He reascended into heaven in the flesh in which He rose again, that He

20   sits at the right hand of the Father, whence He will come *to iudge the living and the dead* (2 Tim. 4.1), and that He is both God and man."

Origen said: "Since the beginning of a debate is the time to declare what the topic of the debate is, I will

25   speak. The whole Church is here listening. It is not fitting for doctrinal differences to exist from church to church, for you are not a Church of falsehood. I call upon you, Father Heraclides: God is the almighty, the uncreated One, who

30 is above all and who has made all things. Do you agree to this?"

Heraclides said: "I agree; for this is what I too believe."

Origen said: "Jesus Christ, *though he was in the form of God* (Phil. 2.6), while still being distinct from God in

35 whose form He was, was God before He came into the body: yes or no?"

Heraclides said: "He was God before."

Origen said: "Was He God before He came into the body or not?"

Heraclides said: "Yes, He was."

40   Origen said: "Was He God distinct from this God in whose form He was?"

2   Heraclides said: "Obviously distinct from the other and, while being in the form of the other, distinct from the Creator of all."

Origen said: "Is it not true, then, that there was a God,

5 the Son of God and only begotten of God, the *first born of all creation* (Col. 1.15), and that we do not hesitate to speak in one sense of two Gods, and in another sense of one God?"

Heraclides said: "What you say is evident. But we too

10 say that God is the almighty, God without beginning, without end, who encompasses all and is encompassed by nothing, and this Word is the Son of the living God, God and man, through whom all things were made, God according to the Spirit, and man from being born of Mary."

15   Origen said: "You don't seem to have answered my question. Explain what you mean, for perhaps I didn't follow you. The Father is God?"

Heraclides said: "Of course."

Origen said: "The Son is distinct from the Father?"

20   Heraclides said: "Of course, for how could He be son if He were also father?"

Origen said: "And while being distinct from the Father, the Son is Himself also God?"

Heraclides said: "He is Himself also God."

Origen said: "And the two Gods become a unity?"
25   Heraclides said: "Yes."
Origen said: "We profess two Gods?"
Heraclides said: "Yes, [but] the power is one."[1]

The Teaching of Origen[2]

Origen said: "But since our brothers are shocked at the
30   statement that there are two Gods, we must treat this
matter carefully, and point out in what respect they are
two, and in what respect these two are one God. Now the
holy Scriptures have taught many instances of two being
35   one; and not just two, but in some cases they have taught us
that more than two and even a great number are one. Our
3   task here is not to take up this problem just to pass over it
quickly but, for the sake of the more simple,[3] to chew on it
5   like meat and instill the doctrine little by little in the
ears of our hearers. There are, then, many things which
are two that are said in the Scriptures to be one. What
Scripture passages? Adam and his wife are distinct beings; Adam is distinct from his wife, and his wife is distinct from her husband. But it is said right in the creation
10   account that the two are one: *For the two shall become one
flesh* (Gen. 2.24; Matt. 19.5). It is thus possible at times for
two to be one flesh. But note well that in the case of Adam
and Eve it is not said that they will be two in one spirit,
15   nor that they will be two in one soul, but that *they will be
two in one flesh*. In addition, the just person, while distinct from Christ, is said by the Apostle to be one in relation to Christ: *For whoever is united to the Lord is one
spirit with him* (1 Cor. 6.17). But is not one of these of a
20   lower or diminished and inferior nature, while Christ is
of a more divine and glorious and blessed nature? Are
they therefore no longer two? Yes, *for the man and the
woman are no longer two but one flesh* (Matt. 19.6), and
25   the just person and Christ are 'one spirit.' Thus, our Savior
and Lord, in relation to the Father and God of all, is not
one flesh and one spirit, but something that is above both

flesh and spirit, one God. For when human beings are join-
30 ed to each other, the appropriate word is 'flesh,' and
when a just person is united to Christ, the word is 'spirit,'
and when Christ is united to the Father, the word is not
4   'flesh' or 'spirit,' but the more prestigious word: 'God.'
That is why we understand *I and the Father are one* (John
10.30) in this sense. In some of our prayers we maintain
5 the duality and in others we introduce the unity, and thus
we do not fall into the opinion of those who, cut off from
the Church, have fallen prey to the illusory notion of unicity (μοναρχίας), abrogating the Son as distinct from the
Father and also, in effect, abrogating the Father; nor do
10 we fall into the other impious doctrine which denies the
divinity of Christ. What, then, is the meaning of such
sacred texts as: *Before me no other god was formed, nor
shall there be any other after me* (Isa. 43.10), and the
text: *I, even I, am he, and there is no god beside me* (Deut.
15 32.39)? In these texts, one is not to think that the unity
refers to the God of the universe in his purity (as the heretics would say) apart from Christ, nor that it refers to
Christ apart from God; but we say that it is just as Jesus
expresses it: *I and the Father are one* (John 10.30).

The Problem Of Prayer

20   "Care must be exercized in the way one speaks of these
things because this subject has been the cause of much agi-
tation in this church. Requests are frequently written for
(doctrinal formulas) to be signed, that the bishop should
sign, and that those who are under suspicion should also
25 sign, and that one should sign in the presence of all the
people so that there will be no further dissension or dis-
pute in the matter. Therefore, with the permission of God,
and secondly of the bishops, and thirdly of the presbyters
30 and the people, I will again give my opinion in the matter. Oblation is constantly made to God the all-powerful
through Jesus Christ by reason of his communication in divinity with the Father. Nor is it made twice but (once) to

God through God. I will seem to speak daringly: in prayer
35 it is necessary to respect the conventions, otherwise one
becomes subject to the text: *Be not a respecter of persons nor*
5 *be in awe of the person of the powerful* (cf. Lev. 19.15) . . .
A bishop thus stands over all. If not, and the conventions
5 are not observed, new problems arise. He who is in one respect a bishop or a presbyter, is in another respect not a
bishop and a presbyter. He who is in one respect a deacon,
is in another respect not a deacon or a layperson. Whoever
is a layperson in one respect, in another respect is not, and
10 does not attend assemblies. If this makes sense, let these
conventions be kept.[4]

Examination of an Objection

"With regard to the divinity, some object that, while
admitting the substantial divinity of Jesus Christ, I did so
15 in such a way that I professed before the Church the resurrection of a dead body.[5] But since our Savior and Lord
did assume a body, let us examine what the body was. The
Church alone, againat all the heresies that deny the resurrection, professes the resurrection of the dead body; for
20 from the fact that the first fruits have been raised from
the dead, it follows that the dead rise. *Christ is the first
fruits* (1 Cor. 15.23); this is why his body became a corpse.
25 For if his body had not become a corpse, able to be
wrapped in a shroud, anointed with spices, and whatever
else is done to corpses, and able to be laid in a tomb—these
are things that cannot be done to a spiritual body. For it is
in no way possible for something spiritual to become a
30 corpse, nor, such as it is, for the spiritual to become insen-
sible. For if the spiritual should become a corpse, we
should have to fear that, after the resurrection of the
dead when our body has been raised according to the word
35 of the Apostle: *It is sown a physical* (ψυχικόν) *body, it
is raised a spiritual* (πνευματικόν) *body* (1 Cor. 15.44), we
6 would all die. *For Christ being raised from the dead will
never die again* (Rom. 6.9). But not only *Christ being*

5 *raised from the dead will never die again*, but also *those
who belong to Christ* (1 Cor. 15.23), having been raised
from dead, will never die again. If you are in agreement
with these points and they are solemnly affirmed by the
people, they shall be codified and definitively fixed.[6]

Intervention of Maximus

"Tell us, Maximus, what else regarding the faith is
there to talk about?"

10   Maximus said: "Would that all were of the same opinion
as I. Before God and the Church I both affix my signature
and condemn. But that I might be totally free of doubt and
incertitude, I do have a particular question to ask. And my
15 brothers know this, for I was saying: 'I need the help of my
brother and to be instructed on this point.' Granted that the
spirit (of Jesus) was handed over to the Father according to
the words: *Father, into your hands I commend my spirit*
20 (Luke 23.46) and that, separated from the spirit the flesh
died and lay in the tomb, how was the tomb opened, and
how do the dead rise?"

Origen said: "We have learned from the holy Scriptures that the human being is a composite.[7] For the Apos-
25 tle says: *May God sanctify your spirit and your soul and
your body, and also: May the God of peace sanctify you
wholly; and may your spirit and soul and body be kept
sound and blameless at the coming of our Lord Jesus Christ*
30 (1 Thess. 5.23). This spirit is not the Holy Spirit, but a
part of the human composite, as the same Apostle teaches
us when he says: *The Spirit bears witness with our spirit*
(Rom. 8.16) for if it were the Holy Spirit, he would not
7   have said: *The Spirit bears witness with our spirit*. So
then, our Savior and Lord, in his desire to save the human
race as he willed to save it, for this reason thus willed to
5 save the body, just as he willed likewise to save also the
soul, and willed also to save the rest of the human being:

the spirit. For the whole human being would not have
been saved if he had not assumed the whole human being.[8]
They eliminate the salvation of the human body by saying that the body of the Savior is spiritual; they elimi-
10   nate the salvation of the human spirit, of which the
Apostle says: *No one knows the thoughts of a human being
except the spirit of the human being which is in him* (cf. 1
Cor. 2.11). Desiring to save the spirit of the human being,
15   about which the Apostle spoke, the Savior assumed also
the human spirit. These three elements were separated at
the time of the passion; they were reunited at the time of
the resurrection. How? The body in the tomb, the in   20
Hades, the spirit committed to the Father. The soul in
Hades: *You do not give up my soul to Hades* (cf. Ps. 16[15].
10; Acts 2.27). If he committed his spirit to the Father, he
25   gave his spirit in deposit. It is one thing to 'make a gift,'
another thing to 'deliver up,' and another thing to 'give in
deposit.' The depositer makes a deposit[9] with the inten-
30   tion of recovering the deposit. Why, then, did He have to
give His spirit in deposit to the Father? This is beyond me
and my ability to understand. For I am not sure enough of
this to affirm that, just as the body was not able to de-
8   descend into Hades, despite the affirmations of those who
say that the body is spiritual, so too was the spirit unable to descend into hell; that is why He gave His spirit
5   in deposit to the Father until He rose from the dead. This
deposit, committed to the Father, He takes back. When?
Not right at the resurrection, but immediately after the
10   resurrection.[10] Witness the text of the Gospel: the Lord
Jesus rose from the dead; Mary met Him and He said to
her: *Do not touch me* (John 20:17). For He wanted those
who touched Him to touch Him in His entirety so that,
15   touching Him in His entirety, they would receive in their
body the benefit of His body, in their soul the benefit of
His soul, in their spirit the benefit of His spirit—*For I
have not yet ascended to the Father* (John 20.17). He
ascends to the Father and then comes to His disciples. He

thus ascends to the Father. For what purpose? To recover His deposit.

Faith and Works

"All the questions regarding the faith that were bothering us have been examined. But we must keep in mind
25 that we are judged at the divine tribunal not on our faith alone as if we did not have to answer for our conduct (cf. James 2.24), nor on our conduct alone as if our faith were not subject to examination. It is from the correctness of both
30 that we are justified; it is from the noncorrectness of both that we are punished for both. But there are some who will not be punished for both but for one of the two; some
9 will be punishedfor defective faith, but not for an incorrect life, while others will not be punished for their faith but will be punished for a life lived contrary to right rea-
5 son. It is my understanding that in the Proverbs of Solomon these two orders of things—I mean what conerns our faith and doctrine and what concerns our life—are spoken of by
10 Solomon in the following manner: *Who will boast of having a clean heart; or who will put himself forward with the claim of being pure of sins?* (Prov. 20.9). The difference
15 in these expressions we take to be this: the "heart" relates to thought, the "sins" relate to deeds. Who *boasts of having a clean heart* not defiled by *false knowledge* (1 Tim.
20 6.20), not defiled by lying? Or *who will put himself forward with the claim of being pure of sins*, of having committed no sin in his practical life? If then we wish to be saved, let us not, in our commitment to the faith, be neg-
25 ligent of our practical conduct, nor, conversely, be overconfident of our conduct. It is from both that we know, understand, believe, and will have our reward and beatitude, or their opposite. For to be punished are not just the horrible
30 and terrible things in both spheres *which should not be mentioned* (Eph. 5.3), but also things commonly thought to be of lesser importance. It is for this reason, it seems, that the Apostle set alongside of the things which are (if one

35 must mention them) abominable, infamous and criminal,
10 also things commonly thought to be of little importance.
What is it he says? *Do not be deceived; neither the im-*
moral, nor adulterers, nor the effeminate, nor homosex-
5 *uals, nor thieves or drunkards or revilers will inherit the*
kingdom of God (cf. 1 Cor. 6.9-10). You see that together
with such enormous evils as homosexuality, effeminate
10 morals, adultery, fornication, he sets drunkenness and abusive speech, sins we all think are of less importance, so
that we might learn that it is not just for the former sins
that we are cast out of the kingdom of God, but also for
15 these which are thought to be less serious. Accordingly,
even if we are all wrong about this, let us not use abusive
language, get drunk, be rapacious or thieving, and also not
commit abominable acts, even if we are mistaken.[11]

"If you have a further question about the rule of faith,
please call it to my attention. In the meantime, we will
continue commenting on the Scripture."

The Question of Dionysius: Is the soul blood?

20 Dionysius said: "Is the soul blood?"[12]

Origen said: "It has come to my ears, and I speak in
full knowledge of the situation, that some people here
25 and in the surrounding regions think that the soul, after
its deliverance from this life, no longer perceives anything but lies in the tomb, in the body. And I recall being
carried away with some vehemence on this matter against
30 the other Heraclides and Celer, his predecessor, indeed
with such vehemence that I wanted to drop the subject and
leave. Nevertheless, it was with honorable intentions
and for the sake of the subject under discussion that he
11 had sent for us. We resumed the discussion. A declaration
was made in which he cleared himself before us as before
God with professions of faith.

"It is a necessary question, therefore, that our dear

5 Dionysius asks. I will first cite the passages which cause
the trouble, so as not to forget any of them, and, God per-
mitting, we will respond to each one in accordance with
10 your request. The vexing passage is: *The soul of all flesh
is its blood*—ἡ ψυχὴ πάσης σαρκὸς αἷμά ἐστιν (cf. Lev.
17.11). This text has terribly disturbed those who do not
understand it. Then there is the text: *You shall not eat the
soul with the flesh: be sure that you do not eat the blood:*
15 *you shall not eat the soul with the flesh* (cf. Deut. 12.33,
Gen. 9.4). This is the really troublesome text; for the other vexing passages are far less emphatic than the thought
20 expressed here. I then, for my part, and praying for assistance in reading the sacred texts (for we need assistance to
keep our thought from departing from the truth). . . I have
25 found that noncorporeal things are given names similar to
all corporeal things. The result is that bodily things refer
to the outer human being, but the homonyms for bodily
things refer to the inner human being. Scripture says that
the human being is two human beings: *Although our outer*
30 *human nature is wasting away, our inner human nature is*
being renewed every day (2 Cor. 4.16); and: *I delight in*
the law of God according to my inner human nature (Rom.
12 7.22). The Apostle everywhere maintains each of these
two human natures in distinction from each other. But it
seems to me that this doctrine was not due to Paul's bold
5 initiative. Rather, having drawn it from the Scriptures
where it was expressed somewhat unclearly, he conceived
and formulated it more clearly. Some people think that it
is a repetition in the creation account when, after the
creation of the human being, we read: *God took dust*
10 *from the ground and formed the human being* (Gen. 2.7).
From this intepretation it follows that what is *in the*
image (Gen. 1.26) is the body and that God is given a
human form, or that the form of God is according to this
15 type. But we are not so mad as either to say that God is
composed of an inferior element and a superior element, in
order to have the *in the image* apply to both, since the *in*
the image refers to God in his entirety, or to say that the

in the image is more perfectly realized in the inferior than in the superior element.[13]

Excursus: Exhortation to the Audience

20 "These problems are rather delicate. We need hearers with a keen mind. I call upon my hearers therefore to be on their guard not to make me liable to the reproach that I am throwing sacred things to dogs (cf. Matt. 7.6), to

25 shameless souls. For those given to bark, the cynics, those given to debauchery and abusive language, all they do is howl like dogs. I must not cast holy things before such

30 people. Thus I call upon my hearers not to make me incur the reproach of casting forth the magnificent pearls which I am attempting to collect, like merchants demon-

13 strating merchandise to those wallowing in the impurities of the body, and thus of doing business with swine (cf. Matt. 7.6). For I would say that whoever is constantly

5 involved with bodily things and wallows in the dirty things of life and has no desire for the pure and holy life,

10 such a person is nothing but a swine. Thus, since *the kingdom of heaven is like a merchant in search of fine pearls* (Matt. 13.45), if I find these beautiful pearls and, after purchasing them at the cost of hard work and night vigils,

15 throw them to pleasure-loving souls and those given to the filthy things of the body and all wrapped up in impurity, I too will have done wrong because I cast pearls

20 before swine (cf. Matt. 7.6). And when the swine receive the pearls, not seeing their beauty or perceiving their excellence, they will stomp on them by reviling what was

25 correctly expressed; and not only do they stomp on the pearls but, turning back, they will revile the ministers of the pearls.

"I beseech you, therefore, be transformed (cf. Eph. 4.20-24; Rom. 12.1-2). Resolve to learn that you can be trans-

30 formed and put aside the form of swine, which describes
the impure soul, and the form of dog which describes the
person who barks and howls and speaks abusively. It is

14 possible to be transformed (even) from serpents. For the
wicked person is addressed: *You serpent and brood of
vipers!* (cf. Matt. 23.33). If, then, we are willing to hear

5 that it is in our power to be transformed from serpents,
from swine, from dogs, let us learn from the Apostle the
transformation that depends on us. This is how he puts it:

10 *We all, with unveiled face, beholding the glory of the
Lord, are being changed into his likeness* (2 Cor. 3.18). If
you were a barker and the Word molded you and changed
you, you were transformed from a dog to a human being.
If you were impure, and the Word touched your soul,

15 and if you offered yourself to be shaped by the Word,
you were changed from a swine into a human being. If you
were a wild beast, on hearing the Word which tames and
domesticates, which changes you by the will of the Word

20 into a human being, you will no longer be addressed: *You
serpent, and brood of vipers* (cf. Matt. 23.33). For if it were
impossible for these serpents, the ones in the soul because
of wickedness, to be changed, the Savior (or John the Bap-
tist) would not have said: *Bear fruits that befit repen-
tance* (Luke 3.8 *par*). When you have repented, you are no

25 longer a *serpent, a brood of vipers* (Matt. 22.33).

"Since then the subject before us is the human being and,
with regard to the soul of the human being, to find out
whether it is blood, and since the subject has brought us to

30 treat in detail the doctrine of the two human beings, and
since we have come to a mystical subject, I appeal to you not
to make me guilty on your account of casting pearls before
swine and holy things to the dogs, of throwing things di-

15 vine to serpents, of giving the serpent a share in *the tree of
life* (Gen 2.9). To spare me from this charge, be transformed,
put away malice, discord, *anger*, quarrelsomeness, wrath,

5 grieving, and duplicity (cf. Col. 3.8), so that there will no

longer *be dissensions among you. but that you (will) be unit-*
ed in the same mind and the same judgment (1 Cor. 1.10).

"I am worried about speaking; I am worried about not
speaking. For the sake of the worthy, I want to speak so as
10 not to be guilty of defrauding of the Word those able to
hear it. Because of the unworthy, I hesitate to speak, for
the reasons mentioned, so as not to throw holy things to
15 dogs and cast pearls before swine. It was for Jesus alone to
know how to distinguish among his hearers between those
without and those within, and thus to speak to those outside in parables and to explain the parables to those who
came into his house (cf. Mark 4.11). This being *outside* or
20 *coming into the house* has a mystical meaning.[14] <*For
what have I to do with judging outsiders?* (1 Cor. 5.12).
Whoever sins is *outside*. This is why those outside must
be spoken to in parables, in case they might be able to
leave the outside and come inside. The coming into the
house has a mystical meaning.> Whoever enters Jesus'
house is his true disciple. He comes in by thinking with
the Church, by living according to the Church. Being
within and *without* are spiritual (πνευματικόν) realities.

25   "You see how long my preamble is to prepare my
hearers. I hesitate to put off speaking, and when I do
speak I change my mind again. What is it I really want?
To treat the matter in a way that heals the souls of my
hearers.

Return to the Problem:
The Two Human Beings and the Principle of Homonymy

30   "In creation, therefore, the human being first created was the one *in the image* (Gen. 1.26) in whom is nothing material.[15] For what is made *in the image* is not made
from matter. *And God said, Let us make man in our image,*
35 *after our likeness; and let them have dominion* and so

16   forth (Gen. 1.26). *And God made man* not by *taking dust*
          from the ground as he did the second time (Gen. 2.7), but
        5 made him *in the image of God* (Gen. 1.27). That Moses was
          not the only one to know that his being *in the image of God*
          is nonmaterial, superior to every bodily substance, but
          that the Apostle also knew this, is shown in his text
       10 which says: *Seeing that you have put off the old human*
          nature with its practices and have put on the new which
          is being renewed in knowledge after the image of its
          creator (Col. 3.9-10).

          "There are, therefore, two human beings in each of us.
          What is the meaning of saying that *the soul of all flesh is*
       15 *its blood* (cf. Lev. 17.11)? This is a great problem. For
          just as the outer human being has the same name as the
          inner, so too with its members; thus one can say that every
          member of the external human being is also called the
          same thing in the inner human being.[16]

       20   "The outer human being has eyes, and the inner human
          being is said to have eyes: *Lighten my eyes lest I sleep the*
          sleep of death (Ps. 13[12].3). This is not talking about
       25 these bodily eyes, nor about bodily sleep, nor about ordi-
          nary death.[17] *The ordinance of the Lord is far-seeing,*
          enlightening the eyes (cf. Ps. 19[18]8-9). It is not just in
          observing the commandments of the Lord that we become
       30 clear-sighted in bodily things, but in observing the divine
          commandments according to the mind (κατὰ τὸν νοῦν) that
          we become more clear-sighted. The eyes of the inner hu-
          man being see more perceptively than we do. *Open my*
          eyes and I will understand the wondrous things of your
17   *law* (Ps. 119[118].18). Is this to say that his eyes are
          veiled? No, but our eyes are our mind. It was for Jesus to
        5 pull back the veil that we might be able to contemplate
          what has been written and understand what has been
          spoken in secret. The external human being has ears, and
          the internal human being is also said to have ears. *He*
       10 *who has ears to hear, let him hear* (Matt. 11.15 and

passim). All had the ears of the external senses, but not all have been successful in having internal ears which are purified. Having ears of the senses does not depend on us,

15 but having internal ears does. For it depends on us to have those (kinds of) ears which make the Prophet say: *Hear, you deaf; and look, you blind. that you may see! And who*

20 *is deaf but my servants? And who is blind but their masters? And the servants of God have become blind* (Isa. 42.18-19). Take note now, that this becoming deaf is our

25 responsibility! What I am saying will apply to all of us. The inner human being must be described so that the blood may be located. That this becoming deaf according to those (inner) ears is indeed our responsibility, hear the

30 declaration of the prophet: *The wicked have been estranged from birth: they have gone astray from the womb, they have spoken lies. Fury is in them like the fury of a*

18 *serpent, like that of an adder which is deaf and stops its ears, and which will not listen to the voice of the charmers and the incantation being addressed to it by an exper-*

5 *ienced man*[18] (cf. Ps. 58[57].3-5). And you, too, who know yourselves to be guilty: if you listen to the word and the *incantation being addressed to you by an experienced man*, and listen to the words of those trying to charm you into

10 repressing your fury and wickedness, and if you then close your ears instead of opening them up wide to hear what is said, then the text: *Fury is in them like the fury of a*

15 *serpent, like that of an adder which is deaf and stops its ears, and which will not listen to the voice of the charmers and the incantations being. addressed (to it) by an experienced man* (cf. Ps. 58[57].3-5) will apply to you.

"The exterior human being smells with his nostrils, perceiving good odor and bad odor, while the inner human being has other nostrils with which to perceive the good

20 odor of righteousness and the bad odor of sins. The Apostle teaches about the good odor when he says: *For we are the good odor of Christ to God among those who are being*

25 *saved and among those who are perishing, to some a frag-*

*rance from death to death, to others a fragrance from life
to life* (cf. 2 Cor. 2.15-16). And Solomon in the Canticle of
Canticles also says, through the mouth of the young maid-
30 ens of the daughters of Jerusalem: *We run after you to the
fragrance of your perfumes* (Cant. 1.4). Therefore, just as
19 we perceive with our nostrils good sensible odors and bad
sensible odors, so too with the inner human being and with
5 someone who has healthy organs for perceiving divine
things, there is a perception of the good odor of righteousness—which the Apostle had—and the bad odor of sins.
What is the bad odor of sins? The Prophet speaks of them
10 in this way: *My wounds grow foul and fester in the face of
my foolishness* (Ps. 38[37].5).

"The outer human being has the faculty of taste, and
the inner human being has the spiritual (πνευματικόν)
15 faculty of which it is said: *Taste and see that the Lord is
good* (Ps. 34[33].8; cf. 1 Peter 2.3). The outer human being
has the sensible faculty of touch, and the inner human being also has touch, that touch with which the woman
with a hemorrhage touched the hem of Jesus' garment (cf.
Mark 5.25-34 *parr*). She touched it, as He testified who
20 said: *Who touched me?* (Mark 5.30). Yet just before, Peter
said to Him: *The multitudes are pressing upon you and you
ask, 'Who touched me?'* (Luke 9.45 *par*). Peter thinks that
those touching are touching in a bodily, not a spiritual
25 (πνευματικῶς) manner. Thus, those pressing in on Jesus
were not touching Him, for they were not touching Him in
faith. Only the woman, having a certain divine touch,
30 touched Jesus and by this was healed. And because she
20 touched Him with a divine touch, this caused power to go
forth from Jesus in response to her holy touch. Hence He
says: *Someone touched me: for I perceive that power has
5 gone forth from me* (Luke 8.46). It is about this healing
touch that John says: *Which we have touched with our
hands concerning the word of life* (1 John 1.1).

"We thus have other hands, about which is said: *May the lifting up of my hands be an evening sacrifice* (Ps 141
10 [140].2). For if I lift up these (bodily) hands, but leave the hands of my soul idle and do not lift them up with holy and good deeds, the *lifting up of my hands* does not become
15 *an evening sacrifice*. I also have different feet about which Solomon is speaking when he commands me: *Let not your foot stumble* (Prov. 3.23).

"In Ecclesiastes there is an unusual text. It will seem meaningless to those who do not understand it; but it is of
20 the wise that Ecclesiastes says: *The wise man has his eyes in his head* (Eccl. 2.14). In what head? For all hu-
25 man beings, even the senseless and the foolish, have bodi- ly eyes in their head. But the wise have the eyes we have been speaking of, eyes which are illumined by the ordi- nance of the Lord (cf. Ps 19[18].9), and they have them in
30 their head, i.e., in Christ, because *the head of man is Christ*, the Apostle says (cf. 1 Cor. 11.3). The thinking faculty is in Christ.

"*My bowels, my bowels are in anguish*, said Jeremiah (Jer. 4.19). In what bowels is he in anguish? Those in
21 which we too are in anguish as they are in labor bringing the people to birth: *my bowels are in anguish. and my bodily senses*, not these but those *of my heart* (cf. Jer. 4.19 and Gal. 4.19).
5 "If I come now to the subtle parts of the body, I see them in an unbodily form in the soul. *Lord, rebuke me not in your anger, nor chasten me in your wrath. Be merciful to*
10 *me, O Lord, for I am weak; heal me, O Lord, for my bones are troubled* (Ps. 6.1-2). What bones of the Prophet were troubled? The constitution of his soul and the firmness of
15 his mind were troubled, and he pleads for the restoration to health of those bones. *Our bones have been scattered in Hades* (cf. Ps. 141[140].7). What bones of the speaker were scattered in Hades? Consider, I ask you, the sinner: look at
20 his frame in the domain of sin, in the place of the dead,

in the domain of evil. You will say of such a person that
25 his bones have been scattered. *All my bones shall say, 'O
Lord, who is like thee?'* (Ps. 35[34].10). These bones talk,
they discuss, say things and perceive God, even though
30 they have no feeling (as the physicians' assistants, who
saw the bones of the patient who does not feel the sawing,
tell us). *All my bones shall say, "O Lord. who is like*
22 *thee?"* (Ps. 35[34].10). All these bones the inner human
being possesses.

"The inner human being has a heart: *Hearken to me.
you who have lost your heart* (Isa. 46.12 LXX). Those
5 people did possess a heart, that of the body, for that
heart does not get lost. For when someone has neglected
the cultivation of his intellectual life, and after too much
10 idleness his thinking capacity has dried up, he has lost
his heart. It is to such a person that the text: *Hearken to
me, you who have lost your heart* is addressed.

"*Even the hairs of Your head are all numbered* (Matt.
10.30). What hairs: Those by which they were spiritual-
15 ly (πνευματικῶς) Nazirites.[19]

"Since you have all these elements of the physical
body in the inner human being, you should no longer have
problems about the blood, which, with the same name as
20 physical blood, exists, just like the other members of the
body, in the inner human being. That is the blood which is
poured forth from a soul; for *He will require a reckoning
for the blood of your souls* (Gen. 9.5). He does not say,
25 "your blood" but, the *blood of your souls*. And, *His blood I
will require at the watchman's hands* (Ezek. 33.6). What
blood does God *require at the watchman's hands* if not
that which is poured forth from the sinner? Just as, when
30 the heart of the foolish man is lost, and it is said: *Heark-
en to me, you who have lost your heart* (Isa. 46.12 LXX), so
23 too does the blood and the vital power flow away from
his soul.

"If one has understood the soul and understood it according to the inner human being, and understood that in it

5 is the *in the image* (Gen. 1.26), it becomes evident how nobly Paul expresses this: *It is better to be dissolved and be with Christ* (cf. Phil. 1.23).[20] Before the resurrection the just person is with Christ and, in his soul, lives with

10 Christ. Hence, *It is better to be dissolved and be with Christ*. But according to those of you who say that the soul lies in the tomb with the body, it did not depart from the body, it does not enjoy repose, it does not dwell in God's

15 paradise, it does not repose in the bosom of Abraham (cf. Luke 16.23). According to those of you who maintain such absurd things, it is not better to be dissolved and be with Christ (Phil. 1.23). For, if the soul is indeed blood, there is no being with Christ just as soon as the dissolution takes

20 place. If the soul lies in the tomb, how can it *be with Christ*? But in my view and that of the word of God, the soul which is freed from troubles and freed from pain, which has been liberated from the body and is able to say:

25 *Now You may dismiss your servant, O Lord, in peace* (Luke 2.29), that soul departs in peace and is in the repose of

30 Christ. Thus it was that the soul of Abraham heard the words: *You shall go to your fathers in peace: you shall be buried in a good old age* (Gen. 15.15). He goes off to join his

24 fathers. What fathers? Those of whom Paul says: *For this reason I bow my knees before the Father from whom (comes) every family* (cf. Eph. 3.14-15). It was in this

5 sense, we think, that Aaron was dissolved (cf. Num. 20.28-29). For in Ecclesiastes it is written of the just person who has fought the good fight and is departing from the prison of the body that *From the house of the prisoners he will*

10 *go forth to be a king* (Eccl. 4.14). And so, I am ready to die for the sake of truth; ard so, in the face of so-called certain death, I scorn it; and so: Come wild beasts! Come crosses! Come fire! Come tortures! I know that as soon as it

15 is over, I depart from my body, I am in peace with Christ. Therefore let us take up the battle, therefore let us take

20 up the struggle, groaning at being in the body, not as if,

once in the tomb, we will be back in the body, but (per-
suaded that) we will be set free and will exchange our
body for something more spiritual. Destined as we are *to
be dissolved and be with Christ* (cf. Phil. 1.23), how *we
groan* (cf. 2 Cor. 5.24), we who are in the body!"

The Observations of Demetrius:
Is the Soul Immortal?[21]

25   As Bishop Philip came in, Demetrius, another bishop, said: "Our brother Origen is teaching that the soul is
immortal."

30   Origen said: "The statement of Father Demetrius has
brought us to the beginning of another problem. He said
that we have stated that the soul is immortal. To this
25   statement I will reply that the soul is both immortal and
not immortal. First, let us carefully define the word
  5 'death' and all the meanings that come from the term
'death.'[22] I will try to present all its meanings, not according to the Greeks, but all its meanings according to holy
Scripture. Perhaps someone more learned than I will
 10 point out still other meanings. Presently, however, I know
of three deaths. What are these three deaths? Someone
may *live to God* and have *died to sin*, according to the
 15 Apostle (cf. Rom. 6.10). This death is a blessed one: one
dies to sin. This is the death which my Lord died: *For the
death he died he died to sin* (Rom. 6.10). I also know an-
 20 other death by which one dies to God. About this death it
is said: *The soul that sins shall die* (Ezek. 18.4). And I
know a third death according to which we ordinarily consider that those who have left their body are dead. For
Adam *lived nine hundred and thirty years, and he died*
(cf. Gen. 5.5).

25   "Since, therefore, there are three deaths, let us see whether the human soul is immortal with regard to these three deaths, or, if not with regard to all three deaths,
30 whether it might still be immortal with regard to some of them. All of us human beings die the ordinary death which we think of as a dissolution. No human soul ever
26 dies this death; for if it did die, it would not be punished after death. *Men will seek death,* it is written, *and will*
5 *not find it* (cf. Rev. 9.6). For the souls being punished will seek death. They will desire not to exist rather than exist to be punished. This is why *men will seek death and will*
10 *not find it.* Taken in this sense, every human soul is immortal. Now for the other meanings: according to one, the soul is mortal and blessed if it dies to sin. This is the death
15 that Balaam was talking about in his prophecy, praying in the divine spirit: *Let my soul die among the souls of the just!* (Num. 23.10). It was about this death that Balaam made his astonishing prophecy and, in the word of God,
20 prayed the most beautiful of prayers for himself; for he prayed to die to sin in order to live to God. This is why he said: *Let my soul die among the souls of the just, and let*
25 *my seed be like their seed!* (Num. 23.10). There is another death, in regard to which we are not immortal; but it is possible for us, through vigilance, not to die this death. And perhaps what is mortal in the soul is not mortal for-
30 ever. For to the extent that it allows itself to commit such a sin that it becomes a *soul that sins* which *itself will die* (cf. Ezek. 18.4), the soul is mortal for a real death. But if
27 it becomes confirmed in blessedness so that it is inaccessible to death, in possessing eternal life it is no longer mor-
5 tal but has become, according to this meaning too, immortal. How is it that the Apostle says of God: *Who alone has immortality* (1 Tim. 6.16)? I investigate and find that Jesus Christ *died for all except God* (cf. 2 Cor. 5.15 and
10 Heb. 2.9). There you have the sense in which God *alone has immortality.*

"Now then, let us take unto ourselves eternal life; let
us take it unto ourselves as best we can. God does not give
15 it to us, but sets it before us: *See, I have set before you life*
(cf . Deut. 30.15; Jer. 21.8). It is for us to stretch forth our
hands by performing good deeds and lay hold of life and
20 deposit it in our soul. This life is Christ, who said: I *am
the life* (cf. John 11.25 and 14.6), this life which is presented to us now in shadow, *but then face to face* (1 Cor. 13.
25 12): *For the Spirit is before our face, Christ the Lord of
whom we say: in his shadow we shall live among the na-
tions* (cf. Lam. 4.20). If the shadow brings to your life so
many good things—the shadow Moses had when he
30 prophesied, which Isaiah had when he saw the *Lord of
Hosts sitting upon a throne, high and lifted up* (Isa. 6.1,5),
which Jeremiah had when he heard the words: *Before I
formed you in the womb I knew you, and before you were
28   born I consecrated you* (Jer. 1.5), which Ezekiel had when
he saw the Cherubim (Ezek. 10.1), when he saw the
wheels (Ezek. 1.15-16), the ineffable mysteries—if the
shadow brings so many good things, what will not our life
5 be when we no longer live under the shadow of life but
will be in life itself! For now *our life is hid with Christ.
But when Christ. who is our life, appears, then* we *also
10 will appear with him in glory* (cf. Col. 3.3-4). Let us
hasten towards this life, groaning and grieving that we
are in this tent (cf. 2 Cor. 5.4), that we are at home in the
15 body. For as long as *we are at home in the body we are
away from the Lord* (cf. 2 Cor. 5.6). Let us, then, yearn *to
be away from the body and at home with the Lord* (cf. 2
Cor. 5.8) so that, being at home with him, we might be-
20 come one with the God of all and His only begotten Son,
finding in all things salvation and blessedness in Jesus
Christ, to whom be the glory and the power for ever and
ever. Amen.

25   **Dialogues of Origen
with Heraclides and his Fellow Bishops
on the Father, the Son, and the Soul**

NOTES

LIST OF ABBREVIATIONS

Cat	Greek Catenae, *PP* fragmenta (see G & N 52-95)
ComJn	Origen, *Commentary on John:* GCS 10 (IV)
Dialogue	Dialogue of Origen with Heraclides and His Fellow Bishops on the Father, the Son, and the Soul (see Bibliography: Sherer)
G & N	O. Guéraud and P. Nautin (see Bibliography)
GCS	Die griechischen christlichen Schriftsteller der ersten drei Jahrhunderte (Berlin 1897–)
Hist.eccl.	Eusebius, *Historiae ecclesiasticae*: GCS 9.1 and 9.2 (II.1 and II.2)
PG	J.-P. Migne, *Patrologiae Cursus Completus*, Series Graeca (Paris 1857–)
PP	*Peri Pascha*: Origen's Treatise on the Passover
Pr	Procopius of Gaza, *PP* fragments (see G & N 52-95)
SC	Sources chrétiennes (Paris 1941–)
Vic	Victor of Capua, *PP* fragments (see G & N 52-95)

SELECT BIBLIOGRAPHY

Hans Urs von Balthasar, "Le Mysterion d'Origène," *Recherches de Science Religieuse* 26 (1936) 513-62; 27 (1937) 38-64; also published as *Parole et Mystère chez Origène* (Paris: Cerf 1957).

_____, *Origen, Spirit and Fire: A Thematic Anthology of His Writings*, trans. R. J. Daly (Washington: Catholic University 1984).

Ulrich Berner, *Origenes, Erträge der Forschung* 147 (Darmstadt: Wissenschaftliche Buchgesellschaft 1981).

Raniero Cantalamessa, *L'Omelia "In S. Pascha" dello Pseudo-Ippolito di Roma* (Milan: Vita e Pensiero 1967).

Bernard Capelle, "Origène et l'oblation à faire au Père par le Fils, d'après le papyrus de Toura," *Revue d'Histoire Écclésiastique* 47 (1952) 163-71.

Enrico Cattaneo, *Trois homélies Pseudo-Chrysostomiennes sur la pâque*, Théologie historique 58 (Paris: Beauchesne 1981).

Henry Chadwick and J. E. L. Oulton, eds., *Alexandrian Christianity* (London: SCM/Philadelphia: Westminster 1954).

Henri Crouzel, *Bibliographie Critique d'Origène* and *Supplément I*, Instrumenta patristica 8 and 8A (The Hague: Nijhoff 1971, 1982).

_____, "La distinction de la 'typologie' et 'allégorie,'" *Bulletin de littérature ecclésiastique* 65 (1964) 161-174.

_____, *Origen: The Life and Thought of the First Great Theologian*, trans. A. S. Worrall (San Francisco: Harper & Row 1989).

Robert J. Daly, "The Hermeneutics of Origen: Existential Interpretation in the Third Century," in *The Word in the World: Essays in Honor of Frederick Moriarty, S.J.* (Cambridge, Mass.: Weston College 1973) 135-43.

_____, "The *Peri Pascha*: *Hermeneutics and Sacrifice*," in *Origeniana Tertia* (Rome: Edizioni dell'Ateneo 1985) 109-117.

Edgar Früchtel, *Das Gespräch mit Herakleides und dessen Bischofskollegen über Vater, Sohn und Seele. Die Aufforderung zum Martyrium*, Bibliothek der griechischen Literatur 5 (Stuttgart: Anton Hiersemann) 1974.

Rolf Gögler, *Zur Theologie des bibliachen Wortes bei Origenes* (Düsseldorf: Patmos 1963).

Octave Guéraud and Pierre Nautin, *Origène. Sur la Pâque, Christianisme antique* 2 (Paris: Beauchesne 1979).

A. Hamman, *The Paschal Mystery: Ancient Liturgies and Patristic Texts*, Alba Patristic Library 3 (Staten Island: Alba House 1969).

R. P. C. Hanson, *Allegory and Event: A Study of the Sources and Significance of Origen's Interpretation of Scripture* (London: SCM 1959).

Marguérite Harl, *Origène et la fonction révélatrice du Verbe Incarné*, Patristica sorbonensia 2 (Paris: Seuil 1958).

Lothar Lies, "Zum Stand heutiger Origenesforschung," *Zeitschrift für katholische Theologie* 102 (1980) 61-75, 190-205.

Gennaro Lomiento, *Il dialogo di Origene con Eraclide ed i vescovi suoi colleghi sul Padre, il Figlio e l'anima*, Quaderni di "Vetera Christianorum" 4 (Bari: Adriatica 1971).

Henri de Lubac, *Histoire et Esprit: L'intelligence de l'écriture d'après Origène*, Theologie 16 (Paris: Aubier 1950).

_____, "'Typologie' et 'Allégorisme,'" *Recherches de Science Religieuse* 34 (1947) 180-226.

Pierre Nautin, *Origène: Sa vie et son oeuvre*, Christianisme antique 1 (Paris: Beauchesne 1977).

Origeniana. Premier colloque internationale des études origéniennes, 1973, eds. H. Crouzel, G. Lomiento, J. Rius-Camps; Quaderni di "Vetera Christianorum" 12 (Bari: Istituto de Letteratura Cristiana Antica 1975).

Origeniana Secunda. Second colloque internationale des études origéniennes, Bari, 1977, eds. H. Crouzel, A. Quacquarelli; Quaderni di "Vetera Christianorum" 15 (Rome: Edizioni dell'Ateneo et Bizzarri 1980).

Origeniana Tertia. The Third International Colloquium for Origen Studies, Manchester, 1981, eds. R. Hanson, H. Crouzel (Rome: Edizioni dell'Ateneo 1985).

Origeniana Quarta. Die Referate des 4. Internationalen Origeneskongresses, Innsbruck, ed. 1985, ed. Lothar Lies; Innsbrucker theologische Studien 19 (Innsbruck/Wien: Tyrolia 1987).

Jean Scherer, ed., *Entretien d'Origène avec Héraclide et les évèques ses collègues sur le Père, le Fils, et l'âme,* Textes et documents 9 (Cairo: Publications de la Société Fouad I de Papyrologie 1949); summarized as SC 67 (Paris: Cerf 1960).

Karen Jo Torjesen, *Hermeneutical Procedure and Theological Method in Origen's Exegesis,* Patristische Texte und Studien 28 (Berlin/New York: de Gruyter 1986).

_____, "Origen's Interpretation of the Psalms," Studia Patristica 17 (Oxford/New York: Pergamon 1982) 944-958.

Joseph Wilson Trigg, *Origen: The Bible and Philosophy in the Third-Century Church* (Atlanta: John Knox 1983).

NOTES

INTRODUCTION

[1]Cf. O. Guéraud and P. Nautin, *Origène sur la Pâque*, (Christianisme antique 2; Paris: Beauchesne 1979) 16-24.

[2]Cf. O. Guéraud, "Note préliminaire sur le papyrus d'Origène découvert à Toura," *Revue de l'histoire des religions* 136 (1946) 99-103.

[3]Cf. J. Scherer, *Extraits des livres I et II du Contre Celse d'Origène d'après le papyrus No. 88747 du Musée du Caire* (Bibliothèque d'Etude 28; Cairo: Institut francais d'Archéologie orientale 1956).

[4]Cf. J. Scherer, *Le commentaire d'Origène sur Rom. III.5–V.7 d'après les extraits du papyrus No. 88748 du Musée du Caire et les fragments de la Philocalie et du Vaticanus Gr. 762: Essai de reconstruction du texte et de la pensée des tomes V et VI du "Commentaire sur l'épître aux Romains"* (Bibliothèque d'Etude 27; Cairo: Institut français d'Archéologie orientale 1957).

[5]Cf. J. Scherer, ed., *Entretien d'Origène avec Héraclide et les évêques ses collègues sur le Père, le Fils, et l'âme* (Publications de la Société Fouad I de Papyrologie; Textes et Documents 9; Cairo: Institut français d'Archéologie orientale 1949).

[6]See above n. 1. For further information about these papyrus discoveries, cf. O. Guéraud, "Note préliminaire" 85-99; H.-Ch. Puech, "Les nouveaux écrits d'Origène et de Didyme découverts à Toura," *Revue d'histoire et de philosophie religieuses* 31 (1951) 293-329.

[7]Cf. Eusebius, *Hist.eccl.* 6.1.1–8.6; 6.14.10–39.5. The most reliable presentation of Origen's life is in pp. 1-58 of H. Crouzel, *Origen: The Life and Thought of the First Great Theologian* (San Francisco: Harper & Row 1989). This book also provides

the most reliable and up-to-date presentation of Origen's thought and writings. For a critical but sometimes adventurous analysis of Eusebius and the other sources for Origen's life, cf. esp. P. Nautin, *Origène: Sa vie et son oeuvre* (Christianisme antique 1; Paris: Beauchesne 1977). On this: R. Daly, "Origen Studies and Pierre Nautin's *Origène*," *Theological Studies* 39 (1978) 508-519. J. W. Trigg, *Origen: The Bible and Philosophy in the Third-Century Church* (Atlanta: John Knox 1984), has been criticized by Crouzel as being one-sided and insufficiently attentive to significant recent developments in Origen studies.

[8]Our main source for the list of Origen's works is Jerome's *Epistle 33* (to Paula). See the works of Crouzel and Nautin mentioned in n. 7.

[9]See H. Urs von Balthasar, "Introduction" in *Origen: Spirit and Fire: A Thematic Anthology of His Writings* (trans. R. Daly; Washington, D. C.: Catholic University 1984) 1-23. See also below in Notes to the Text, n. 52 (on *PP* 43.6).

[10]The catenae have 5 quotations from the *PP* corresponding, when added together, to about 6 pages of the Tura codex. Procopius has 12 quotations corresponding to almost 11 pages. From Victor of Capua comes one quotation (in Latin) which enables us to reconstruct 9 otherwise missing lines from the bottom of p. 32. For full detail, see G & N 52-95. When the text is not witnessed to by the Tura codex but only by one or other of these other sources, we follow G & N's custom of printing the translation in indented format with the source indication in the margin.

[11]See Tertullian, *De baptismo* 19.1.

[12]For the text, see O. Perler, *Meliton de Sardes: Sur la Pâque (et fragments)* (SC 123; Paris: Cerf 1960); ET: A. Hamman, *The Paschal Mystery: Ancient Liturgies and Patristic Texts* (Alba Patristic Library 3; Staten Island: Alba House 1969) 26-39. For the early Christian passover treatises and homilies in general, see also R. Cantalamessa, *L'Omelia "In S. Pascha" dello Pseudo-Ippolito di Roma: Ricerche sulla Teologia dell'Asia Minore nella Seconda Metà del II Secolo* (Milan: Vita e Pensiero 1967); R. Daly, *Christian Sacrifice: The Judaeo-Christian Background before Origen* (Studies in Christian Antiquity 18;

Washington, D.C.: Catholic University 1978) 373-378; E. Cattaneo, *Trois homélies Pseudo-Chrysostomiennes sur la pâque comme oeuvre d'Apollinaire de Laodicée: Attribution et étude théologique* (Théologie Historique 58; Paris: Beauchesne 1981).

[13]It is cited in a much later Byzantine *Paschal Chronicle:* PG 92, 80C-81A (see G & N 98).

[14]Philo, *On the Special Laws* 2.145-47; *Moses* 2.224; *Who Is the Heir* 192; *On the Migration of Abraham* 25; *Questions and Answers on Exodus* 4-19.

[15]For the text: P. Nautin, *Homélies Paschales I: Une homélie inspireée du traiteé sur la pâque d'Hippolyte* (SC 27; Paris: Cerf 1950). What appears to be a direct quotation from Hippolytus is also found in the Byzantine *Paschal Chronicle* (PG 92, 80B-C).

[16]τὸ δὲ πάσχα οὐκ ἔφαγεν ἀλλὰ ἔπαθεν.

[17]*ComJn* 10.18(13): GCS 10 (IV) 189.27-29.

[18]See R. Daly, "The Hermeneutics of Origen: Existential Interpretation in the Third Century." *The Word in the World: Essays in Honor of Frederick Moriarty, S.J.* (Cambridge, Mass.: Weston College 1973) 135-43 .

[19]See K. J. Torjesen, "Origen's Interpretation of the Psalms" (*Studia Patristica* 17/2; Oxford/New York: Pergamon 1982) 944-58; *Hermeneutical Procedure and Theological Method in Origen's Exegesis* (Patristische Texte und Studien 28; Berlin/New York: de Gruyter 1986).

[20]See n. 14 above .

[21]As Christians, we cannot avoid asking whether Origen gives sufficient weight to the historical reality of the Incarnation, on the one hand, and the this-worldly bodiliness of Christian life on the other. His apparent concern to counteract an excessively narrow interpretation of the passover in terms of the passion can explain why he may not appear to do so in this treatise. But also across the whole body of his work, it seems to be the case, when examined from a traditional Christian perspective, that the Platonizing cast of his thinking does not allow him to give a properly full emphasis to these central Christian realities.

[22]*ComJn* 10.13(11)–19.14: GCS 10 (IV) 182.8–191.4.

[23]*ComJn* 10.13(11): GCS 10 (IV) 183-184.
[24]*ComJn* 10.14(11): GCS 10 (IV) 185.11.
[25]*ComJn* 10.14(11): GCS 10 (IV) 185.12-16.
[26]*ComJn* 10.15(12): GCS 10 (IV) 186.1-4.
[27]*ComJn* 10.15(12): GCS 10 (IV) 186.4-7.
[28]*ComJn* 10.16(13): GCS 10 (IV) 186.18-22.
[29]*ComJn* 10.17(13): GCS 10 (IV) 187.18-22.
[30]*ComJn* 6.51(32)—60(38): GCS 10 (IV) 160-69.
[31]*ComJn* 10.17(13): GCS 10 (IV) 187.22–188.9.

[32]It is also noteworthy that this passage, despite the prominence of John 6:50-56, is not about the Eucharist. What comes to the fore is a deeply spiritualized theology of the sacramentality of the word of God in its many manifestations. The fact that the idea of the sacramental reception of the eucharistic bread of life apparently occurred to Origen at most only fleetingly in this context suggests a number of conclusions. But first, a nonconclusion: one cannot conclude from this that the sacramental Eucharist, as this came to be understood by later Christian theology, is totally unknown to Origen or rejected by him. This would be an argument from silence from *one* passage (although there also many others like it in Origen). It would also be a somewhat anachronistic application of a later theology to an earlier figure. Nevertheless, the very fact that Origen, so skilled at bringing in ideas and insights from any and all sources, did not make even one obvious allusion to the sacramental Eucharist in this whole section, suggests at least that this doctrine did not hold a strong place in his imagination and consciousness, or at least that he did not feel constrained to emphasize it on every possible occasion.

[33]*ComJn* 10.17(13): GCS 10 (IV) 188.1-14.

[34]*ComJn* 10.18(13): GCS 10 (IV) 188.24: literally, "boiling" spirit (*zeonti pneumati*). This could be an allusion to the boiling water which the eastern rite priests pour into the chalice before communion and which, for the 14th century Byzantine theologian Nicolas Cabasilas—*A Commentary on the Divine Liturgy* (London: S. P. C. K., 1960)—was a symbol of the Holy Spirit. Cf.

C. Blanc, *Origène. Commentaire sur Saint Jean*, vol. 2 (SC 157; Paris: Cerf 1970) 444-45, n. 1.

[35]*ComJn* 10.18(13): GCS 10 (IV) 188.15--189.1

[36]*ComJn* 10.18(13): GCS 10 (IV) 189.12-13.

[37]*ComJn* 10.18.(13): GCS 10 (IV) 189.14-21.

[38]The term "exodus" not only recalls the departure from Egypt and looks ahead to beatitude, in Origen it also often signifies death (cf. C. Blanc in SC 157, p. 449, n. 4).

[39]*ComJn* 10.18(13): GCS 10 (IV) 189.21-33.

[40]τὰ περὶ τοῦ χρόνου τοῦ πάσχα—*ComJn* 10.19(14): GCS 10 (IV) 190.27-28. We do not know if Origen ever wrote this technical discussion of the date of the passover. The *Peri Pascha* does not fit this description, for it concentrates not on the date itself but on a more detailed theological issue related to this discussion: that the passover is a type not of the passion of Christ, but of Christ Himself and of His *passage* (and that of the Christians) to the Father.

[41]*ComJn* 19.14(14): GCS 10 (IV) 190.30–191.4.

[42]The general idea is that when the "spirituals," having put aside their (psychic) souls, will have become pure spirits again, they will enter into the nuptial chamber and will be given as spouses to the angels who surround the Savior. Cf. C. Blanc in SC 157, p. 453; E. Corsini, *Commento al Vangelo di Giovanni di Origene* (Classici della filosofia; Turin: Unione Tipografico - Editrice, 1968) 74; 407 n. 25; 531-532 n. 70. See further Irenaeus, *Adv. haer.* 1.1.12: W. Harvey, *Sancti Irenaei Libros quinque adversus Haereses* (Cambridge: Typis Academicis 1858) 1.58-59; Clement of Alexandria, *Excerpta ex Theodoto* 64: GCS 17 (III) 128,15-19.

[43]See Scherer, *Entretien* 2-5.

[44]See Scherer, *Entretien* 17-38, 47-49.

[45]See Scherer, *Entretien* 50-58; O. Chadwick, *Alexandrian Christianity* (Philadelphia: Westminster 1954) 430-36.

[46]See B. Capelle, "Origène et l'oblation à faire au Père par le Fils, d'après le papyrus de Toura," *Revue d'histoire ecclésiastique* 47 (1952) 163-71.

[47]On the theme of the resurrection in Origen see H. Crouzel, "Les propheties de la resurrection selon Origène" in *Forma Futuri. Studi in onore del Cardinale Michele Pellegrino* (Turin: Bottega d'Erasmo 1975) 980-992; "Mort et immortalité selon Origène," *Bulletin de littérature ecclésiastique* 79 (1978) 19-38, 81-96; Basile Studer, "La resurrection de Jesus d'après le 'Peri Archôn' d'Origène," *Augustinianum* 18 (1978) 279-309; Bruno Salmona, "Origène e Gregorio di Nissa sulla resurrezione dei corpi e l'apocatastasi," *Augustinianum* 18 (1978) 383-88.

[48]On Origen's anthropology in general, and on his understanding of the tripartite composition of human beings, see J. Dupuis, *L'esprit de l'homme. Etude sur l'anthropologie religieuse d'Origène* (Collection Museum Lessianum, section théologique 62; Bruges: Desclée de Brouwer 1967); H. Crouzel, "L'anthropologie d'Origène dans la perspective du combat spirituel," *Revue d'ascétique et de mystique* 31 (1955) 364-385.

[49]This raises the question of esoteric teaching in Origen, as might also the conclusion of the *Peri Pascha* (49.34 to 50.8). Origen always had in mind at least one, and usually two or more, of the following general types of readers/interpreters of Scripture: (1) the Jews whom he depicts as clinging to the literal/historical meaning, thus rejecting Christ (since, e.g., the lion has not in fact laid down with the lamb); (2) the gnostics (γνωστικοί) who clung to the literal meaning in order the more easily to discredit and reject the scriptures not to their liking; (3) the simple faithful (πιστικοί) who clung to the literal meaning as the word of God, but in a way that left them open to the ridicule of the heretics; (4) the perfect or spiritual (πνευματικοί) who were willing and able to search behind the literal meaning for the more true spiritual meaning. This necessarily involves a certain esotericism in the general sense, but not in the sense that Origen consciously formulated his teaching in such a way that only the initiate could understand it. It seems, on the contrary, that Origen repeatedly got into trouble for saying and writing things that were disturbing to the simple faithful. See below n.51 and H. Crouzel, *Origène et la "connaissance mystique"*

(Collection Museum Lessianum, section théologique 56; Bruges: Desclée de Brouwer 1961).

[50]See H. Crouzel, *Théologie de l'image de Dieu chez Origène* (Théologie 34: Paris: Aubier 1956); G. S. Gasparro, "Doppia creazione e peccato di Adamo nel 'Peri Archon': fondamenti biblici e presupposti platonici dell'esegesi origeniana," in *Origeniana Secunda* (ed. H. Crouzel and A. Quacquarelli; Quaderni di "Vetera Christianorum" 15; Rome: Edizioni dell'Ateneo 1980) 57-67.

[51]Much has been written about Origen's exegesis. We recommend especially H. de Lubac, *Histoire et Esprit: l'intelligence de l'Ecriture d'après Origène* (Théologie 16; Paris: Aubier 1950) and H. Crouzel, *Origen* (San Francisco: Harper & Row, 1989) 61-84. For a much briefer treatment, see R. J. Daly, "Translator's Foreword" in *Origen. Spirit and Fire: A Thematic Anthology of His Writings* by H. U. von Balthasar (Washington: Catholic University 1984) xi-xviii; "The Hermeneutics of Origen: Existential Interpretation in the Third Century" in *The Word in the World* (Cambridge, MA: Weston College Press 1973) 135-143.

ON THE PASSOVER

[1]"The brethren—οἱ αδελφοί" is a term commonly used by Origen to refer to his fellow Christians. In this case, Origen is refuting a position held by heretics (cf. his strong rejection of Heracleon's position in the *Commentary on John* which we mentioned above towards the end of the introduction to the *Treatise on the Passover*). However, Origen is also aware that this is an error shared by many fellow Christians. Hence this term of respect.

[2]The Greek verb "to suffer—πάσχειν" is practically identical with the Greek word for "passover—πάσχα."

[3]For "passage," Origen uses the word διάβασις 5 times (1.18, 22; 2 17; 4 18,22) and the word ὑπέρβασις twice (45.14; 47.33). He

seems to use them synonymously, and there is not enough evidence to determine whether there is any significance in the fact that he uses διάβασις when his primary context is exodus, and ὑπέρβασις when his primary context is the resurrection/ascension of Christ. Only a few later writers attempt to distinguish between them, referring ὑπέρβασις to the "passing over" of "the destroyer" or "angel of death" in Exod. 12.13,23. Cf. E. Cattaneo, *Trois homélies pseudo-Chrysostomiennes sur la pâque* (Théologie historique 58; Paris: Beauchesne 1981) 9-16.

[4]Origen's words contain a double meaning which expresses an important reservation. He normally uses the term "perfect Hebrews" or "true Hebrews" to refer to Christians (e.g., cf. *Exhortation to Martyrdom* 33: *Ancient Christian Writers* 19.173, or *Origen* [The Classics of Western Spirituality; New York: Paulist 1979] 63). Thus he seems to be reminding us here that Hebrews will indeed know that "passover" means "passage," but only Christians will know what this really means. A similar reservation seems to be expressed in the phrase "if there really is a circumcision" in *PP* 29.3.

[5]In this paragraph, Origen states his main thesis: the passover is not just something that happened in the past, "the passover still takes place today" in the lives of the Christians, in their spiritual itinerary, in their "passage."

[6]Above and beyond the geographical place in Palestine, "Holy Land" has two meanings for Origen: the state of perfection which the soul enters into in principle here below, and the state of perfection and beatitude to which it comes in the life beyond (cf. *Homily on Numbers* 26.4 beginning).

[7]This is one of the numerous formulas with which Origen refers to the spiritual meaning contained in or behind the literal or historical meaning of the biblical text. Thus, on the following page, "the history" (*PP* 4.6), i.e., the Jewish passover, is contrasted with "the true passover" (*PP* 4.17 to 18), i.e., the "passage" of the Christian into a new way of life through baptism.

[8]"The *first month*." In terms of modern historical reckoning, the Jewish year began at the autumnal equinox (the month of

Nisan). The inconsistency on this point is probably caused by the fact that the postexilic calendar made Nisan the beginning of the year, while the older agricultural calendar (which long remained in competition with the new calendar) had the beginning in Tishri. Origen, of course, did not have access to the historical tools which would have enabled him to unravel such inconsistencies, which he interpreted as signals to search for the true, i.e., deeper or spiritual meaning.

[9]Origen now spends a full two and one-half pages (*PP* 4.36 to 7.14) to explain that the words "This month shall be for you the beginning of months" (Exod. 12.2) were spoken not to the whole people but only to Moses and Aaron. For they alone had fully renounced the life of this world and entered into the way of perfection.

[10]At this point Origen spends 5 more pages (more than one-tenth of the treatise, from 7.15 to 12.21) on the words "beginning—ἀρχή" and "first—πρῶτος" in order to explain that what is *"first"* is always *"beginning,"* but that *"beginning"* is not always *"first."* The importance of this for Origen becomes clear when he explains, toward the end of this section, that "beginning" is associated with the Son, but "first" is reserved for the Father who alone is unbegotten. This clearly reflects the theological situation of a time when Christians were deeply concerned to safeguard the unity of God together with the distinction of the divine persons, esp. Father and Son, but were not yet fully aware of the dangers of subordinationism. For example, cf. below, the opening section of the *Dialogue with Heraclides.* Origen at times sounds (to our ears) subordinationist. Whether he actually was or not is most difficult, and perhaps even impossible to determine. One must keep in mind how and when the Christological and trinitarian doctrines were developed and formulated. A great deal of what the post Arian age condemned as subordinationist was, in Origen's time, taken for granted as orthodox Christian theology. This section of the *Treatise on the Passover* is a typical example of Origen's theological method. Apart from his summary of the rule of faith at the beginning of *On First Principles,* he rarely formulates and expounds doctrine as such.

Rather he quotes and expounds scripture (from both testaments), drawing doctrine and his understanding of it from the texts. Modern hermeneutics, of course, can point out that this works only because Origen already has an at least implicit doctrinal and speculative synthesis to draw upon. Origen is not unaware that he has such a synthesis which he refers to as the "rule of faith." Cf. R. P. C. Hanson, *Origen's Doctrine of Tradition* (London 1954/New York 1956); *Tradition in the Early Church* (London 1962). Here Origen "draws" his doctrine from Gen. 1.1 (*PP* 8.7 to 29), Rev. 22.13 (*PP* 10.3 to 11.4), John 1.1 (*PP* 11.5 to 31) and Gen. 49.3 (*PP* 11.31 to 12.5).

[11]Our translation here, within the brackets, summarizes the meaning of what is, for the most part, a conjectural reconstruction of 5 defective lines (*PP* 7.17 to 21).

[12]Origen apparently has in mind the other beings created before this world, such as angels and spirits, and probably also the other worlds which he thinks may have existed before this one.

[13]Gap in the text of 1 1/2 lines; the phrase in parenthesis is a conjectural reconstruction.

[14]Gap in the text of about 2 lines; the phrase in parenthesis represents the meaning which seems to result from a conjectural reconstruction.

[15]Our translation of 10.20 to 24 represents a conjectural reconstruction.

[16]In *PP* 12.25 to 16.4, Origen returns to his main theme, offering three arguments to support his affirmation that the passover is not a type of the passion. (1) The passover lamb is sacrificed by holy people, but Christ by criminals and sinners (12.25 to 13.3), as he had already pointed out in his Commentary on John 10.16(13): GCS 10 (IV) 186.28-30. (2) The scriptural directives about roasting and eating the flesh of the passover lamb are not fulfilled in the passion, but they are fulfilled in the life of the Christian (13.3 to 14.13). (3) The Savior Himself (in John 3.14, alluding to Num. 21.8-9) sees not the passover but the lifting up of the serpent in the wilderness by Moses as the prefiguring of His passion (14.25 to 15.11).

[17]"The saints" refers to the sanctification of the Jewish people in Jos. 5.12 (cf. *Homilies on Joshua* 6.1: GCS 30 [VIII] 321-4) by circumcision before celebrating the passover and crossing the Jordan to the Promised Land (cf. also Num. 9.6). "The Nazirites" Origen apparently identifies or associates with the passover lamb the "one male lamb a year old without blemish" (Num. 6.14) prescribed as a sacrifice for the Nazirite at the end of his period of consecration.

[18]Origen is obviously developing the idea of the universal priesthood of the faithful which, in general, is also much closer to the core of his concerns than is the official, hierarchical priesthood. Here, he probably intends a Christian application of the teaching of Philo: "But at the passover, here spoken of, the whole people together is honored with the priesthood, for all of them act for themselves in the performance of the sacrifice" (*Questions and Answers on Exodus* 1.10; cf. R. Daly, *Christian Sacrifice* [Studies in Christian Antiquity 18; Washington, D.C.: Catholic University 1978] 410-11).

[19]Origen will later provide more detail on just how the Christian is to offer this passover sacrifice which is Christ. As in his earlier Commentary on John, he interprets the eucharistic sermon in John 6 (here John 6.53) as referring to the spiritual eating of the Word—*ComJn.* 10.17(13): GCS 10 (IV) 187.22–189.9. The necessity of eating this Word in order to "have life" is seen as the true fulfillment of the necessity of eating the passover in order not to be "cut off from the people" (Num. 9.13) or "touched by the Destroyer" (Heb. 11.28). Origen's use here of John 6.53 in an exclusively spiritualized sense does not of itself exclude the possibility of a sacramental conception of the Eucharist in his thought. What is actually being rejected here is a crassly literal eating (cannibalism) of the flesh of Jesus. This is the literal interpretation of "the Jews," and is the reason why, as Origen sees it, they reject the Word. One must keep in mind that, for Origen, the literal meaning of such sayings as "I am the light" refers to the physical phenomenon of light. The metaphorical meaning obviously intended by the evangelist (which modern exegesis tends to call the literal meaning) is classified by Origen

as the spiritual meaning. This is what Origen has in mind when he asserts that some biblical texts have no literal (or historical) meaning at all. Origen thought customarily in Word-eucharistic rather than in sacramental-eucharistic terms. Were we to project our theological concerns onto Origen's thought, his reaction, doubtless, would be to classify a eucharistic interpretation of John 6 as part of its spiritual meaning.

[20]In Num. 21.8-9 Moses is commanded to set the bronze serpent "on a pole" or to set it up "as a sign—ἐπὶ σημείου" (LXX). To get the phrase "hung on the wood," Origen conflates this text (as did also Tertullian in *Against Marcion* 3.18, suggesting a common tradition) with Deut. 21.22-23 where the criminal accursed by God is hung "on the tree —ἐπὶ ξύλου."

[21]Origen has thus paused briefly to insert a point that is central to his whole vision of Christian life, the necessity of proper dispositions. Christ's crucifixion is of no profit to Christians except to the extent that they realize it in themselves by the conduct of their lives.

[22]Origen's brief description of the passover rite contains something not found in Exodus or anywhere else in the Old Testament: the ceremony of dedicating the lamb in which the names of the persons for whom the lamb is to be sacrificed are mentioned (*PP* 16.26 to 30). But this ceremony is contained in the Mishnah tract *Pesahim* 5.3; 6.6; 8.1; 8.3–H. Danby, *The Mishnah* (Oxford University 1933) 141-47, which was being codified in Origen's time. He may have learned about this from the "Hebrew teacher" he sometimes mentions, or perhaps even from more direct knowledge of passovers still being celebrated according to the old rite.

[23]The top halves of pages 17 to 32 are missing. What remains is numbered from the bottom of the page (-1 = bottom line; -5 = 5 lines from the bottom, etc.).

[24]Origen is apparently following the interpretation of Philo, *On the Preliminary Studies* 89-96, which took the number 10 as the perfect number and referred it to God to whom the lamb was to be offered. But Origen modifies this to make the reference specifically to Christ.

[25]In this section, Origen does exactly what Hippolytus does in jumping to Exod. 12.6 to explain the regulation about keeping the lamb until the fourteenth, before returning to explain the rest of Exod. 12.2. He explains, first, the interval between taking the lamb and sacrificing it (*PP* 17.-5 to 19.2) and, second, why the lamb is sacrificed on the evening of the fourteenth (19.-14 to 21.7). First, he does not, of course, follow Hippolytus' interpretation of the interval as referring to the time Jesus was held prisoner between His arrest and crucifixion. Instead, as he does so often in this treatise (and elsewhere), he takes his lead from Philo (*On the Preliminary Studies* 106) who saw the interval as signifying the soul's need to progress to perfection before being able to sacrifice symbolically the passover lamb. But Origen both Christianizes this with an allusion to the time of the catechumenate (*PP* 18.5 to 10) and fills it out by also referring the interval of five days to the five spiritual senses of the inner human being (one of his favorite themes). *PP* 18.15 to 19.2 is also a good example of the exciting biblical-theological richness of his thought which so captivated the great Fathers who came after him. Second, enough of pages 19 to 21 remain to show that Origen interprets the evening of the fourteenth as essentially the fifteenth, the lamb being slaughtered after sundown. Thus the lamb was sacrificed with a perfect full moon, symbolizing the "true light" (John 1.9) which illumines our guiding intellect—(ἡγεμονικόν 21.5) enabling us to sacrifice and eat the true lamb.

[26]In thus associating the passover prescription of a "lamb for each household" with the gospel accounts of the multiplication of the loaves, Origen is possibly alluding to one of his favorite ideas, i.e., that people are found in different degrees of perfection according to the extent to which each one participates in the Logos.

[27]Hippolytus (cf. Pseudo-Hippolytus, *Homily* 19; SC 27.149-51) saw in these words a reference to the two natures of Christ: "perfect" = from heaven, "one year old" = from earth. Origen, however, refers all three of these qualities (without defect, courageous, fulfilled) to the perfection of Christ. Thus Origen

seems to take pains to avoid a reference to the humanity and historical Incarnation of Jesus, even though he could probably do so here without weakening his basic line of interpretation. Since such instances are not uncommon in Origen, one can see how the question could arise whether Origen gives sufficient attention to the Incarnation.

[28]Hippolytus does not even comment on this, but for Origen it is important, for it allows him to allude to his doctrine (developed esp. in the early parts of his *Commentary on John*) on the various names of Christ which correspond to the various levels of one's spiritual advancement.

[29]"Seven loaves of barley"—a mistake by Origen (there are no "seven loaves of barley" anywhere in the New Testament)—which he later corrects in Book 9 of his *Commentary on Matthew* written ca. 248.

[30]The conflation of these two texts into one, specifically the addition of Rev. 7.17, allows Origen to bring in his teaching on the spiritual senses.

[31]This catena fragment is all that remains of a section of some 15 lines in which Origen probably alluded to his interpretation of the parable of the workers in the vineyard (Matt. 20.1-15) in which he sees the five times at which laborers are sent into the vineyard as symbols of the five epochs of history: Adam, Noah, Abraham, Moses, and finally, Christ, who comes toward evening at the eleventh hour. Cf. *Commentary on Matthew* 15 32: GCS 40 (X) 446.23–447.11. Cf also 1 John 2.28 and Origen's comment in *Commentary on Matthew* 11.1: GCS 40 (X) 34.21-23.

[32]In the time of Origen, the word "faith" was often used to signify baptism.

[33]What can be pieced together and reconstructed of this section (*PP* 27 mid to 30 top) leaves us with a brief description of the three major modes of exegesis with which Origen had to deal: (1) the Jews eat the flesh raw, following only the letter of Scripture; (2) the heretics cook the flesh, but with water, i.e., they mix strange doctrine with the Scripture; (3) the Christians, who have the true circumcision, eat the flesh (= Word of God),

which is now possible because it has been roasted with the fire of the Holy Spirit .

[34]The theme of good and bad water is apparently what is developed in these missing lines. Cf. how Origen develops this theme in *Homily on Genesis* 1.2: GCS 29 (VI) 2.21–5.20; and 6.5: Ibid. 75.15–76.8. The similarity of imagery and biblical allusion indicates that the *Treatise on the Passover* has in mind the same kind of development.

[35]The meaning of this sentence depends on the double meaning of "ἀναπέσοντες—falling upon" (*PP* 31.14) in order to eat, and "resting upon" as in John 13:25 where the Beloved Disciple "was resting—ἀναπεσών" his head on the breast of Jesus.

[36]Here Origen agrees with Hippolytus (cf. Pseudo-Hippolytus, Homily 29; SC 27.155) in relating parts of the lamb to the humanity as well as to the divinity of Christ.

[37]The sole source for this paragraph is a Latin fragment from Victor of Capua.

[38]Origen apparently does not, as does Hippolytus (cf. Pseudo-Hippolytus, *Homily* 30; SC 27.157), refer the prohibition againat breaking the bones of the passover lamb to the passion of Christ, but to his own favorite theme of Christ as the nourishment of souls. In addition, we know from the *Commentary on John* that Origen understands "break no bone of it" as a prohibition against breaking "the unity of the Spirit that is in all the Scripture" *ComJn* 10.18(13): GCS 10 (IV) 189.12-13; cf also GCS 10 (IV) 334.1-12 and *Commentary on Matthew* 10.22: GCS 40 (X) 31.11-13.

[39]The following paragraph contains so much of Origen's theological vision that it would take a book to comment on it. Here we must be content with simply pointing out that his strict interpretation of Matt. 22.14: "Many are called, but few are chosen," refers just to this world. In the end, his soteriology is universalistic; he expects the others to be saved in the world to come (cf. *On First Principles* 1.6.1; 2.3.3; and *Homily on Jeremiah* 7.2).

[40]Origen follows a widespread early Christian tradition in referring "loins girded" to the need to control the sexual instinct.

But what is perhaps most significant in this passage is its apparent reference ("the married man who eats the passover") to the sacramental Eucharist. Elsewhere in the *Peri Pascha*, such phrases as "eating the flesh of the Lamb" and the repeated quotation of the eucharistic verses from John 6 make perfect sense when interpreted in a fully spiritualized way, i.e., as signifying the eating of (= believing, accepting and living out) the Word of the Lord. Here, however, "*to pascha trogon*— 'chewing' the passover" (because it uses the same verb as in John 6.54-58) suggests an intentional reference to the sacramental Eucharist. This does not exclude the possible, indeed likely, simultaneous validity of a spiritualized meaning for these words. But the converse would also seem to be true: in those numerous places in the *Treatise on the Passover* where Origen speaks in a spiritualized sense of eating the flesh of the Lamb, it would be rash to exclude from his fertile mind the possibility, and even intention, of a sacramental meaning. One must keep in mind that he never directly excluded the eucharistic meaning, and that in a treatise in which he often did exclude possible meanings.

[41]Thus, instead of emphasizing, as did Hippolytus (cf. Pseudo-Hippolytus, *Homily* 34; *SC* 27.157-59), the contrast between Moses being ordered to take off his shoes and the command to eat the passover with sandals on, thus symbolizing the difference between the Old Testament and New Testament, Origen, apparently more aware of the dangers of the gnostic tendency to separate the two testaments, stresses the compatibility of the two commands. The same concern to emphasize the similarity rather than the contrast between the testaments is also obvious in the final section of Part One, *PP* 38.5 to 39.6.

[42]Origen has at times been accused of denying the bodily resurrection. Unfortunately, his treatise on the resurrection which seems to precede *On First Principles*, and also seems to have been one of the works which precipitated reactions against him in Alexandria, is not extant. A passage such as this, however, shows how unwise it is to assume that he denied the resurrection of the flesh.

[43]Putting "staffs in their hands" (Exod. 12.11) into the mouth of Paul is another instance of an error presumably caused by quoting from memory while dictating. This passage also contains interpretations which we can only describe as rather strained. But such, too, are fairly typical of Origen; they illustrate how extensively his contemporary (or personal) existential referent, i.e., his own situation-in-the-church, influences the meaning he finds in scripture.

[44]For Hippolytus, the staff symbolized the rod of Jesse, via the text of Isa. 11.2 (cf. Pseudo Hippolytus, *Homily* 35: *S C* 27.159). But for Origen (as for Philo, *Allegorical Interpretation* 2.89) it symbolized the rod of correction.

[45]We have commented above in the introduction on the disproportionate brevity of Part Two (39.9 to 50.8). Since he does not wish to provide support to proponents of the passover/passion line of interpretation, Origen does not have much material left, especially since he has already generously interlarded his exegesis of Exod. 12.1-11 with his spiritual interpretation of the passover, i.e., Christ's "passing over" to the Father and the salvation of the soul through Christ. In his Part Two, Origen is content to allude to what has already been treated, and then move on quickly to new material, especially to that part of Christ's passing over which He accomplished, or accomplishes, after His death. This helps account for the elliptical intensity of Part Two, which, in turn, makes it one of the most exciting passages in Origen's writings.

The introduction to Part Two recalls the basic principles of Origen's understanding of the passover: (1) the passover is taking place now; the Hebrew passover does not prefigure the past events of Christ's bodily life, but Christ Himself now saving souls. (2) It is not just the prophetic words of the Bible that refer to the future, but also the actions related or prescribed in the Bible. In these too knowledge is written (*PP* 40.10 to 12). This is knowledge (ἐπιστήμη) in the Platonic sense, i.e., knowledge of the invisible realities which are the realities of God and the soul. This is the kind of knowledge which "the great prophet" (*PP* 40.13) i.e., Moses, had when setting down the legislation for celebrating the passover.

[46]This seems to be an allusion to Col. 2.9 which says of Christ: "In him the whole fulness of deity dwells." But Origen replaces "deity" with "unicity—μοναρχία."

[47]Cf. the *Commentary on Matthew: Commentariorum Series* 45: *GCS* 38 (XI) 90.26-28 where Christ is called "our sabbath and our repose." Origen apparently draws the two titles from Matt. 11.28: "Come to me, all who labor and are heavy laden, and I will give you rest."

[48]According to a widespread cosmological view, which is notably that of the *Ascension of Isaiah*, Origen apparently thinks that beyond the visible world which is composed of 7 heavens is also an invisible world also composed of 7 heavens, of which the first 6 are inhabited by the different orders of angels and the seventh by the Son of God (G & N 139 n.101).

[49]According to the etymology of the word "Israel" as "the man who sees God."

[50]Power (δύναμις) was a common designation for angels in the New Testament.

[51]Origen is apparently comparing the passions to a flock. The lintel is reason (the head of the flock which controls its members). The doorposts evoke the desires which enter the soul through the concupiscible power, and the reactions which go out of the soul by the irascible power. (Cf. *Selecta in Exodum* 12.22: *PG* 12.285A; G &N 140).

[52]This passage (*PP* 43.7 to 47.27) is a striking example of Origen at his best, moving, in a kind of biblical-theological, midrash-like stream of consciousness from one image or idea or text to another, often without pausing to make the connections explicit, and thus articulating in a short space an intensely aesthetic as well as intellectual and spiritual vision of Christian reality. One is not accustomed to hear the word "aesthetic" in connection with Origen, and he is indeed known for paying no great attention to niceties of style and matters of external beauty. But one cannot help think that it may be precisely the aesthetic quality of those impressively frequent passages, above

all in the commentaries and homilies, where, so to speak, "it all comes together," that explains his massive influence on the mind and spirit of so many of the great Fathers to come after him.

[53]Origen plays on the themes suggested by the etymology of "Egypt": oppression, darkness (*PP* 43.6 to 21) and residence in a strange land (43.21 to 30). The "prophet" (43.22) stands, of course, for Moses. Pharaoh, as becomes clear in the course of the passage, stands for the devil.

[54]The Christian apologetics of Origen's time (e.g., of Justin, Tertullian, Eusebius) applied this to the contemporary situation of the Jews who, from the time of Hadrian, were prohibited from entering Jerusalem.

[55]According to the etymology of "Jerusalem" as "vision of peace." The connection with justice was probably suggested by Isa. 54.14 (Septuagint) addressed to Jerusalem: "Your children shall live in great peace; and in righteousness you shall be established."

[56]A significant and, for Origen, typical conflation of two quite distinct texts into one quotation.

[57]Origen seems to be thinking in the context of Adam's sin in paradise. The word "childishness—νηπιότητα" (*PP* 44.30) confirms this since it appears to echo the idea of Theophilus of Antioch, also taken up by Irenaeus, that Adam was, in age, still a baby when he sinned (cf. G & N 145).

[58]Behind this is Origen's view, common among the Platonically oriented early Christian thinkers, that the human being had a tripartite composition: body, soul, and spirit. In paradise, the soul was free between body and spirit. Sin in general (and in particular the sin committed in paradise) comes (came) from the soul leaning more (or giving itself more) to the things of the body than to those of the spirit.

[59]This passage (45.4 to 29) develops from the etymology of "Hebrews" as "migrants."

[60]I.e., not just Pharaoh, but also (and symbolized by him) the devil, prince of darkness, prince of this world, etc.

[61]Another instance of Origen's custom of conflating several texts into one.

[62]I.e., turned back towards the true homeland of the soul.

[63]I.e., without gnosis, the knowledge of the spiritual meaning of Scripture.

[64]Origen had ended Part One at Exod. 12.11a. He now interprets the second half of v. 11. Like Hippolytus (cf. Pseudo-Hippolytus, *Homily* 58-61: SC 27.187-189) he also describes Christ descending into Hades to free the souls of the just waiting there for Him to lead them up to heaven. This does not necessarily support the passover/passion line of interpretation, and indeed is quite consistent with his own passover/passage line of interpretatlon. In this instance, therefore, he is content to make use of his presumed source.

[65]See Ps. 24[23].7 and 9.

[66]The final sentence of this paragraph serves as a brief summary of Part Two.

[67]This may be an allusion to the phenomenon of esoteric teaching. See above, Introduction, n. 49.

DIALOGUE WITH HERACLIDES

[1]The "dialogue" with Heraclides has come to an end. He appears no more. Subsequently, three other bishops, Maximus (6.8), Denis (10.20) and Demetrius (24.24) speak briefly in what basically turns out to be an expository and exhortatory treatise by Origen.

[2]This section (2.28 to 4.19) is an excellent example of Origen's method of drawing his doctrine from a concatenation of scriptural texts from both testaments. It also begins to illustrate the problem, which was becoming acute at this time, of working towards a more adequate formulation of doctrines which were not explicitly contained in the words of Scripture.

[3]On the various audiences Origen usually had to keep in mind, the simple, the perfect, the gnostics, and the Jews, see above, Notes to the Introduction, p. 94 n. 49.

[4]Origen does not seem to be talking here about personal prayer, as he was, e.g., in his *Treatise On Prayer* (see *Ancient Christian Writers* 19), but the official prayer of the Church, the eucharistic oblation (προσφορά–4.30) offered by its official ministers. Hence the importance of agreement on how one is to pray. However, the garbled state of the final 10 lines of this section (5.1 to 10) precludes certainty about this or any other interpretation of them. Neither the copyist nor the reviser seem to have been able to make sense of these lines. Our translation is conjectural and attempts primarily to preserve the flow of meaning in a way that is generally consistent with Origen's customary way of discussing such matters.

[5]Christ's resurrection and the general resurrection of all Christians are closely connected in Origen's mind. This passage is typical of the way he passes easily from one to the other. E.g., see *DePrin* 2.8.4 and the literature cited in the Notes to the Introduction, pp, 93-4 n. 47

[6]The procedure seems to have been that, by (or at) the end of the synod, the doctrinal decisions and agreements would have been formulated and been accepted by the congregation.

[7]On Origen's tripartite anthropology (body-soul-spirit), see above, Notes to the Introduction, p. 94 n. 48.

[8]Origen's insistence on the salvation of the *whole* human being became one of great importance for the development of orthodox Christian theology.

[9]Origen's use of the word "deposit—παρακαταθήκην" in this passage, as distinct from "giving a gift" or "handing over/delivering up" is carefully chosen, as the reader (see also the following note) will discover.

[10]Origen conceives of Christ's resurrection and work of redemption as having several stages or "moments" and as not being complete until He has rejoined the Father and sent down the Spirit. See *ComJn* 6.57 and the extensive discussion of this theme by Cecile Blanc, *Origène, Commentaire sur S. Jean.* Tome 2 (SC

157) 57-58, 88-101. However, the ingenious interpretation of *Do not touch me* which now follows in this dialogue is not found in the commentary. It is important for Origen to stress this point in order to support his argument (which he does not here develop— perhaps because of the presence of the "simple faithful") against those who see the highest "baptism" in Christ's bloody death rather than, and more precisely, in His personal, giving- and-receiving relationship to the Father. See E. Früchtel, *Das Gespräch* 61-62.

[11]From Origen's *Homily on Jeremiah* 20: GCS (III) 180-81 it seems that this otherwise puzzling phrase refers to the loving divine "deception" by which sinners are saved from discourage- ment by not being given the understanding to see that they are rightly condemned not just for the serious sins mentioned in 1 Cor. 6.9-10, but also for much less serious sins.

[12]This question apparently arose from an excessively literal interpretation of the Septuagint version of Lev 17:11 which caused some of the simple faithful to doubt the immortality (and spirituality) of the soul. See above, Introduction to the *Dialogue*, pp. 22-24.

[13]This passage (see also below 15.30 to 16.13) is typical of how Origen will draw a spiritual meaning from the apparent in- consistency between Gen. 1.26 and 2.7. Modern scholars, knowing that 1.26 comes from the Priestly Writer and 2.7 from the Yah- wist, might easily become disenchanted with Origen's appar- ently outrageous eisegesis. We should not allow such after-the- fact discrepancies revealed by modern exegesis to deter us from testing the theological validity of what Origen is saying.

[14]The following 5 lines within the brackets were added at the bottom of this page of the codex by a second hand, with an indication that they are to be inserted at this point.

[15]See n. 13 above.

[16]For Origen's doctrine of the outer and inner human being and of the five spiritual senses which was also taken up and handed on by Augustine, see Karl Rahner, "The 'Spiritual Senses' Ac- cording to Origen" in *Theological Investigations* 16 (New York: Seabury 1979) 81-103, and Hugo Rahner, "Le debut d'une doctrine

des cinq sens spirituels chez Origène," *Revue d'ascétique et de mystique* 13 (1932) 113-15.

[17]Origen comes back to the different types of death in the final section of the dialogue.

[18]Throughout this passage, Origen seems to be thinking of himself as the "experienced man" to whom one should listen.

[19]Judging from similar ideas expressed in Fragment 211 of *Commentary On Matthew*: GCS 41 (XII) 101, Origen may be thinking of hairs as ideas pointing towards God which Christ as head plants in us.

[20]This passage through 24.24, which seems to form a natural ending to the work, is, together with the final paragraph, a fine example of Origen's extempory homiletic rhetoric.

[21]At this point, Origen might well have swung into the concluding doxology (with which he was accustomed to end his homilies), but Demetrius' observation gives him the opportunity to hold forth a bit longer.

[22]See Above, Introduction, p. 24.

INDICES

1. OLD AND NEW TESTAMENTS

2. GENERAL INDEX

A

Aaron, 31, 32, 79
abominable, 69
Abraham, 32, 48, 54, 56, 79, 102
Adam, 57, 63, 102, 107; Adam's sin, 107
adoption, 52;
adultery, 68
aesthetic, 106
Alexander of Jerusalem, 3
Alexander Severus, 3
Alexandria, 2, 3, 104
Alexandrian, 8, 10
allegory, allegorical, 3, 6, 8
Alpha, 34
anagogical, 52
angel of death, 95
angels, 105
anoint, 39, 47, 53, 65
anthropology, 94
Antioch, 3
antitype, 16, 36, 37
Apocalypse, 34
Apollinaris of Hierapolis, 5, 8;
Apollinarism, 20
apologetics, 106
Apostle, the, 25, 30, 32, 36, 43, 44, 47, 48, 51, 65, 66, 68, 70, 71, 73, 75, 80, 81
apostles, 48, 50
apostolic interpretation, 15
appetite, 49
Arian, Arianism, 20, 97
Ascension of Isaiah, 105
ascension, 9, 95
ascent, 10
Asia, 7
assembly, 20, 32, 42, 53
Athens, 3
athlete, 49
Augustine, 110
autumnal equinox, 96

B

bad odor of sins, 75
Balaam, 81
Balthasar, H. Urs von, 86, 90, 95
baptism, baptized, 8, 11, 96, 102, 109
barley loaves, 5, 42
Bassus, 21
beasts, 43
beatitude, 68, 93, 96; blessedness, 81, 82
beginning, 33, 34, 35, 97
belief, 2
Beloved Disciple, 102
Berner, U., 86
Beryllus, 21
biblical interpretation, 9, 10
birth, 32
bishops, 2, 61, 64, 82
bitter herbs, 14, 17, 44
Blanc, C., 92, 93, 109
blessings, 32
blind, blindness, 54, 74
blood, 13, 17, 21, 23, 24, 30, 47, 52, 53, 69, 72, 74, 78, 79
Boanerges, 33
bodily, bodiliness, 10, 11, 15, 23, 70, 71, 74, , 76, 77, 91. 105
bodily-historical, 11
body, 23, 24, 61, 65, 66, 67, 69, 77, 78, 79, 80, 82, 107, 108; of Christ, 22, 46
body, Christ's, 22
boiled, boiling, 14, 17, 44, 92
bondage, 58
bone, bones, 14, 18, 47, 77, 103;
breaking of, 14
Bostra, Synod of, 21
bowels, 77
bread, 13, 40, 42; of angels, 14; of life, 13
breast, 45, 46
brethren, 95
bronze serpent, 99

114

T

taste, 39, 45, 76
teaching, 21
temple, 40
tent, 82
Tertullian, 106; *Against Marcion*, 99; *De baptismo*, 90
Testaments, two, 13; New, 47, 101, 104, 105; Old, 47, 100, 104
Theoctistus, 3
theologians, 2
theological method, 97
Theophilus of Antioch, 107
thighs, 45, 46
thinking faculty, 77
thirst, 44
Tishri, 96
tithes, 48
tomb, 65, 66, 67, 69, 78, 79
Torjesen, K. J., 88, 91
tortures, 79
touch, touching, 39, 76
transform, transformation, 71, 72
translation, 2, 18, 25, 108
tree, 99
tribunal, divine, 67
Trigg, J., 88, 90
trinitarian, 20, 97
tripartite anthropology/composition of human beings, 22, 94, 107, 108
Tura, 1, 2, 19, 90
type, types, typological, 6, 10, 15, 36, 37, 58, 70, 93, 98

U

unbegotten, 35, 97

unbodily form, 77
unicity of God, 20, 53, 63, 105
unity of God, 62, 97
universalism, 103
universe, 64
unleavened bread, 13, 30, 14, 17, 44; feast of, 36
unworthy, 72

V

Valentinian, 21
Victor of Capua, 5, 90, 102
vigils, 71
vineyard, 102
visible, 53; visible world, 105

W

water, 44; 102
wild beast(s), 72, 79
wilderness, 98
wine vats, 40
wisdom, 35; Book of, Wisdom, 35
wise, 76, 77
Witch of Endor, 1
within, without, 72
Word, 13, 22, 35, 62, 72; of God, 45
works, 46
world, 43, 48; of reason 8, 10; of sense 8, 10; to come 16; transient, 55; visible, 105
worldly, 16; underworldly, 14
worship, 2, 20
worthy, the, 72

Y

Yahwist 109

DATE DUE

DEC 12 '97			
JUN 24 '99			
NOV 2 8 2000			
APR 1 3 2004			
OCT 2 8 2004			